St. Joseph's Table Cookbook

100s of Years of Old-World
Family Cooking

St. Joseph's Table Cookbook
By Bro. Gary Joseph, s.F.m.

100s of Years of Old-World Family Recipes
Edited by Debbie Moss
Published by *Servants of the Father of Mercy, Inc. - Mercy Books*
1544 MORSE AVE STE A, VENTURA, CA 93003
Tel. (310) 595-4175

Internet: www.ServantsoftheFather.org - Email:
Contact@Servants of the Father.org
All proceeds benefit the *St. Joseph's Inn Serving 80,000 +
Homeless in So Cal and Beyond*

Copyright © 2017 *Mercy Books* – Servants of the Father of Mercy, Inc.

The books theme, introductory pages, all photographs, overall compilation and content of this publication copyrighted and published by arrangement with the author.

All rights reserved.

This book may not be reproduced in whole or in part,
in any form, by Photostat, microfilm, or any other means,
or incorporated into any informational retrieval system,
electronic or mechanical without written permission of the
copyright holder, *Mercy Books*.

Get in touch with the author to schedule a group presentation or speaking engagement by sending an email request to Contact@ServantsoftheFather.org.

Digital Cookbook ISBN: 978-0-9833816-5-5

U.S. $29.95 (Hardcover Binder)
Dimensions: Width is 7 inches by 9 ¼ inches tall. There are 146 pages, weighing 1.15 pounds.
ISBN 13: 978-0-9833816-4-8
ISBN 10: 0-9833816-4-8

Published October 1, 2017

FOREWORD TO THE KINDLE EDITION

The title suggests hundreds of years of old-world cooking. However, in actuality this cookbook touches upon thousands of years of ancient recipes and ingredients still used today by chefs in restaurants and those creating every-day family cooking at home. In the opening chapter "Appetizers" connect with the fact that we are still smashing and blending guacamole just about the same way the Aztecs and Mayans did hundreds of years ago. Also, the recipe for hummus has been traced to ancient Egyptian records that show the humble chickpea as crushed, pulverized and eaten for thousands of years.

Most interesting is the chapter on "Breads". Why? This wholesome food has always been the "staff of life" tracing as far back as 4,000 BCE. Bread making can be traced, understood and continues to inspire us from many ancient writings of the Bible - Old and New Testaments as well as other non-Biblical but historical works. In the tab on "Breads" check out the fact that the ancient street vendors of Rome sold Castagnaccio, a flatbread made from chestnut flour and topped it with roasted pine nuts. You will discover other ancient street vendor foods made today like zepoles San Gennaro-style and other focaccia flatbreads topped with olive oil, rock salt and rosemary.

Lastly, the modest bean has been known to be a standard in cooking for thousands of years. You will discover its varied use throughout this cookbook from European and Asian to Mexican cuisines. Be sure to read up on "Lupini Beans" and their importance today. The beans are the yellow legume seeds of Lupinus genus. They are traditionally eaten as a snack food after being pickled in a saltwater brine. Lupinis are primarily known in the Mediterranean basin. FYI, the beans are the highest in protein and lowest in carbohydrates among the legumes family. The bean is extremely bitter unless rinsed methodically for ten days and stored daily in the saltwater brine. Roman street vendors sold Lupinis with beer similar to snacking on Edamame (edible soybean) and Saki in modern-day Asian restaurants.

I hope this cookbook will inspire you to connect further with our rich old-world culinary cultures that have so much to offer your family and friends by way of nutrition, taste, flavor, color, texture, fun and community. If you do not understand a term or something else in the cookbook, remember, there is always Google just waiting to help you. Want to know more about how to role, fry, buy, dice, whip, bake or make something? Don't hesitate to go to YouTube. More than likely someone has posted a 3 to 5-minute video to help you! Can't find an ingredient in your local market? Amazon.com has it and will deliver to you within 48 hours!

Prayers and Blessings!

Bro. Gary Joseph

The Chef's Frugal Tips

You can keep your precious cargo of produce - such as fruits, roots, and vegetables fresh for weeks by investing a little preparation time - preferably, as soon as you (and your family) arrive home from the grocery store. Invite everyone to help by learning about the preparation of fresh, safe, and healthy food. Making it a group activity is where the fun comes in.

Also, be sure to invest in two portable refrigerator/freezer thermometers. Assure the long-term freshness of produce by keeping the refrigerator in the "green" zone at 38 to 42 degrees Fahrenheit. Anything warmer is dangerous when it comes to long-term, bacteria-free produce, dairy, and meats. Place the other thermometer in the freezer and always keep it in the safe "blue" or "white" zone.

1. Raspberries, blackberries, blueberries, cherries, grapes, etc. - While at the market, be careful to pick berries that are firm, colorful, and free of black spots and mold. At home, use a small to medium-sized colander to rinse each pack of berries under cold running water. You can also immerse the berries (colander and all) in a clean kitchen sink filled one quarter of the way with cool water. Drain and wash the berries a second time. Shake off excess water from the berry-filled colander and place the fruit in a small to medium-sized bowl, lined with double or triple sheets of paper towels. Stored in a refrigerator, they will keep fresh for up to two weeks. Use them for toppings on yogurt, cold cereal, hot oatmeal, fresh-baked cobbler, berry muffins, pancakes, and more.

2. Cilantro, parsley, green onions, chives, etc. - While at the market, be careful to pick herbs that are crisp, full of body, rich in color, no signs of wilting, and fairly clean. Place one bunch of herbs in a medium-sized colander. Rinse under cold running water and/or soak in a sink filled halfway with water. Drain and wash a second time. Shake off excess

water and dry well with 6 paper towels. Be sure to remove any dead material. Next, use scissors (ideally a pair dedicated to the kitchen), to trim any brown stem bottoms and brown leaves. Then, gently wrap the herbs in two fresh, clean paper towels. Insert them (paper towels and all) in a one quart Ziploc Slider Bag. Squeeze out excess air, form a vacuum, and seal tight. Place in your refrigerator, ideally in a center spot away from vents that can harm and freeze them. Place in a bin used only for organizing herbs, onions, garlic bulbs, sweet potatoes, carrots, celery, and roots. You will not have to purchase these herbs again for as long as four weeks. They stay fresh that long!

3. Bib lettuce, Romaine, Leafy Red, Iceberg, Endive, Swiss Chard, Collard Greens, Dandelion Greens, etc. - While at the market, be sure to pick lettuce that is crisp, not wilted, and fairly free of dirt and decayed leaves. At home, place each type of lettuce in a sink filled with a generous amount of cold water. Then, separate the heads of lettuce. Remove all wilted or bad leaves and wash the fresh leaves a second time. Gently shake off excess water. Dry the leaves in six to 12 sheets of paper towels. Gently wrap leaves in a sheet of four paper towels and insert into a one-gallon Ziploc Slider Bag. Squeeze out excess air, form a vacuum, and seal tight. Place in the refrigerator on a middle or lower shelf away from vents that can harm and freeze them. The greens will keep for four to five weeks, possibly longer. They will be ready for the next salad, sauté of greens and beans, soups or garnishes for appetizers, or meat platters.

4. Onion and garlic bulbs - While at the market, be sure to pick onions and garlic bulbs that are free of the black mold that usually begins to grow at the bottom of the bulb. If the mold is visible at the market, it won't be long before it spreads and kills the other bulbs in the batch. After picking large and plump garlic heads, move on to onions. Yellow onions are rich in flavor and great for everyday recipes - they are also the least expensive. White onions are milder and work well in salads and delicate sauces, like the white Bechamel sauce made for creamed vegetables

and Eggs Benedict. Red onions work well with red cabbage dishes, salads needing color, cold vegetable platters, Greek Feta salads, and garnishes. Red onions fade and lose color when cooked and usually are not a good choice for sautés and frying. Upon arriving home, lightly peel off each onion's excess, paper-like skins. Place them in a one-gallon Ziploc Slider Bag, and then place the bag in a Tupperware bin in the refrigerator. Repeat the same step for the garlic, but do not pull the garlic heads apart. All you need to do is lightly clean off the excess "paper."

5. Russet potatoes, red potatoes, yams, sweet potatoes, gold potatoes, etc. - Assuming you have selected firm potatoes at the market, once you arrive home it's time to prepare them for many weeks of safe-keeping until they are gone. Large potatoes, like yams and russets, should be washed in the kitchen sink. Then, let them dry for a few hours, or even overnight on the dish rack. Once dried, store them in a bowl somewhere in the kitchen. Smaller potatoes, like the reds and golds in five-pound bags, can be stored on a cold kitchen floor or in the pantry. Check on them every few days and throw away any that are going bad so they don't destroy the others.

6. Apricots, peaches, plums, pears, etc. - When fruits arrive in season on the farms, they are picked early to allow for travel time to their final selling spot. So, upon arriving home wash the fruit in generous amounts of water. Place in a fruit bowl on the kitchen counter or table for one to three days, until the fruit is slightly soft to touch. This is when it will be its most tasty and juicy. Then, immediately store the fruit bowl in the refrigerator to enjoy as a snack, to make homemade jam, or as creative additions to lettuce-based and fruit salads.

7. Oranges, tangerines, lemons, limes, etc. - Wash the fruit thoroughly and let it dry on the dish rack for a few minutes. Next, place in a fruit bowl and immediately refrigerate. They will stay fresh in a refrigerator for four to six weeks, and sometimes longer.

8. Carrots - Leave carrots in a closed bag and pull out what you need, as you need it. Do not open the bag or expose the carrots to the refrigerator atmosphere. This will cause rapid wilting and the carrots will turn to mush!

9. Celery - Wash celery in generous amounts of running water. Use your finger to rub dirt off the rips. Use a paring knife to cut off any brown bottoms and/or tops. Next, cut each clean celery stalk into thirds and place the pieces, slightly wet, into one-quart Ziplock Slider Bags. Tuck in one or two clean paper towels around the celery. This helps to squeeze air out so the bag can be sealed tightly. For weeks to come, the celery will be fresh and ready for midnight snacks using peanut butter, or cream cheese stuffing, or as an appetizer using a little dish of olive oil, sea salt,

10. Mushrooms - Fungi are porous and will absorb water like a sponge and become slimy, so do not wash mushrooms. Instead, leave them in the package until you need them. The Mushroom Growers' Association recommends cleaning them with a dry or slightly damp cloth. Then, slice and incorporate them into your recipe as needed. When frying mushrooms, place them in a nonstick frying pan with a mixture of 1/2 stick butter and 1/8 cup olive oil. They crisp well with bursts of great, woodsy flavor. Do not salt mushrooms until after they have been fried.

11. All-purpose flour, wheat, rye, and rice flour all preserve well in a cool dark cupboard, closet, corner or cellar. To prevent hatching of any eggs that may be in flour, keeping it in the refrigerator during the warm months is another effective method for pest control and to maintain freshness. Store baking yeast in the refrigerator as well.

St. Joseph's Inn and Table, a Tradition of Mercy

Soon, when the homeless have surgery in California hospitals, they will have a place to come "home" and recuperate at the *St. Joseph's Inn*. They receive daily nutrition at the *St. Joseph's Table* Scandinavian Smorgasbord, family-style dining in our *Gardens Restaurant*. Through your generous donations for this cookbook and Bro. Joseph's book, *"Proof of the Afterlife 2,"* 100% of all funds support the *St. Joseph's Inn* and the 80,000 + homeless we serve in Southern California and beyond. May we always remember that our Lord was born homeless in a manger. St. Joseph took the holy family and lived homeless on the road to Egypt for many years. Lastly, Jesus was buried homeless in a borrowed tomb. The souls in Purgatory are homeless too. May we open our hearts and pockets with generous donations of alms for the *Servants of the Father of Mercy* homeless family. You can donate online at www.ServantsoftheFather.org or by U.S. mail. Send to, *Servants of the Father of Mercy*, Inc., 1544 Morse Avenue, Suite A, Ventura, CA 93003. To request our publications by phone call: (310) 595-4175.

The Story Behind the St. Joseph's Table and Inn

The *St. Joseph's Inn*—by opening our doors to the poor, middle-class, and rich—carries on the hundreds of years of tradition behind the March 19th feast and *St. Joseph's Table*. In Sicily, Saint Joseph is regarded as their Patron saint. In many Italian-American communities, thanks is given annually to Saint Joseph (San Giuseppe) on March 19th for preventing a famine in Sicily during the Middle Ages. According to legend, there was a severe drought at the time, and the people prayed to St. Joseph to bring them rain. They promised that if he answered their prayers, they would prepare a large feast for the poor to honor him. The rain did come, and the people of Sicily prepared a large banquet. The white bean was the crop that saved the population from starvation and it remains a traditional part of Saint Joseph's Day tables. Inviting the poor to your home and giving food to the needy is a Saint Joseph's Day custom to this very day.

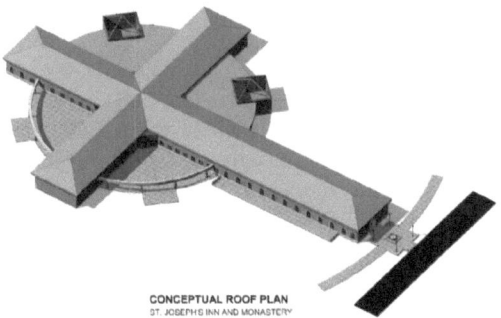

CONCEPTUAL ROOF PLAN
ST. JOSEPH'S INN AND MONASTERY

St. Joseph's Table Cookbook
100s of Years of Old-World Family Recipes

About the Author
The author, Bro. Gary Joseph lives in Southern California where he serves a community of 80,000 + homeless - delivering food, water, clothing, love, hugs and more with a team of 200 lay volunteers. All proceeds from his books *"St. Joseph's Table Cookbook"* and his near-death testimony book, *"Proof of the Afterlife 2"* go to the *Servants of the Father of Mercy* homeless mission - the *St. Joseph's Inn* - a hotel conference center offering at no charge a recuperation home for homeless individuals discharged from Southern California hospitals after surgery.

"Like Us"!
Be sure to "Like" us, the *Servants of the Father of Mercy* and Bro. Gary Joseph - we're located on Facebook, Twitter, Linkedin, and Blogger at www.HomelessInAmerica.BlogSpot.com and on the Internet at www.ServantsoftheFather.org and www.ProofoftheAfterlife.com.

Table of Contents

Appetizers & Beverages 1
Soups & Salads. 13
Vegetables & Side Dishes 27
Main Dishes. 45
Breads & Rolls 67
Desserts 83
Cookies & Candy 97
Parties, Picnics & Family Gatherings 105
Index 115

Recipe Symbols

Award Winning	Diabetic	Freezes Well
Heart Healthy	Holiday	Hot & Spicy
In Memory	International	Quick & Easy
Slow Cooker	Specialty	Vegetarian

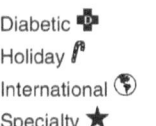

Appetizers & Beverages

APPETIZERS & BEVERAGES

AVOCADO DIP 🍎
(Guacamole)

Maggie Cervantes
Serves 4

- 3 large ripe avocados chopped (split in half and use a spoon to scoop out contents)
- 1 fresh lemon - Squeeze juice from the lemon and pour it over the chopped avocados
- 2 ripe, medium-size tomatoes chopped
- ¼ cup finely chopped white or red onion
- ⅓ cup finely minced, fresh cilantro leaves
- 1 fresh lime - Squeeze juice from the lime and set aside
- Sea salt and fresh ground pepper to taste

Blend all ingredients with a wooden spoon until smooth. Retain the lime juice and pour over the dip just before serving. Then garnish with fresh cilantro on top. Serve with pita bread or tortilla chips.

Note: When eating guacamole, you're consuming history that dates back to the 1500s. The Aztec empire created this spread with the same ingredients that local restaurants use today. The Aztecs called this saucy spread "ahuaca-mulli" which translates to "avocado-mixture" or "avocado-sauce."

CELERY APPETIZER PLATTER ♥
(Stuffed Celery with Cream Cheese)

Paula Grappo

1 large pack Philadelphia Cream Cheese
1 pack Lipton Onion Soup Mix
4 tablespoons whole or skim milk
1 head celery washed, trimmed, dried and cut

In a medium mixing bowl, combine all ingredients. Using a fork, mash cheese, soup mix, and milk until it can be whipped with a tablespoon and become smooth and creamy. Add a drop more milk if necessary. Using a knife, stuff 4- to 6-inch celery sticks. Lightly sprinkle paprika on the sticks to give them color before serving. Arrange celery on an appetizer platter and garnish with small bowls of black and green olives, sweet baby dill gherkins, Mezzetta Porcini hot peppers, and other bottled or fresh vegetable appetizers. Cover the celery and store it in the refrigerator until ready to serve. Place the appetizer platter out for company with small plates, cocktail napkins, and colorful toothpicks.

Note: Paula makes this stuffed celery platter one day ahead of time for Thanksgiving, Christmas, parties, weddings, anniversaries and for other special occasions like picnics and family gatherings. If you make it in advance, be sure to cover with a lot of plastic wrap to keep the celery and cream cheese from drying out in the refrigerator.

CUCUMBER YOGURT SAUCE ⊛
(Cucumber Raita)

Bro. Joseph
Serves 4

2 cups plain yogurt
1 small cucumber peeled, seeded and shredded or finely cut in slivers
3 tablespoons sugar
2 tablespoons fresh minced mint
1 teaspoon dried cumin
1 clove minced garlic (optional)

Combine all ingredients and place them in a small serving bowl, then chill anywhere from one hour to overnight. If the yogurt separates with water on top, gently lay a few sheets of clean paper towels on top for a few minutes. Garnish with fresh mint and serve with your favorite Indian curry chicken, shrimp or pork.

Note: Raita can be used as a dip for naan bread or as a salad. In India it is especially popular during the summer months—as it helps to beat the heat!

EGGPLANT APPETIZER ★
(Appetizer di Melanzane)

Mary D'Amico

2 medium-size eggplants
1 cup apple cider vinegar
1 small bottle olive oil
¼ cup fresh minced garlic
1 small bottle dried oregano
1 small bottle red pepper flakes
6 New Ball or Mason small jelly jars sterilized in boiling water (jars only)
Sea salt

Using a long, sharp kitchen knife, very carefully slice the eggplant as thinly as possible (do not peel). In a large frying pan, bring vinegar to a low bubbly boil. Add enough slices of eggplant and "fry" on each side for a minute or two. Using a slotted spoon, spread the cooked slices out on a meat platter to cool. Drizzle a little olive oil into the bottom of one canning jar. Next, alternate layers of eggplant and minced garlic with a pinch of the following: sea salt, red pepper flakes, oregano, sea salt and a mini splash of olive oil. Continue this process until one jar is completely filled. Place a lid tightly on the completed jar of eggplant appetizer and store in the refrigerator. The longer the eggplant marinates, the better it gets. Because of the vinegar, this appetizer may be kept in the refrigerator almost indefinitely, until it's all eaten up by your family and friends.

Note: Both Aunt Mary (Paula's sister) and my mom made this Italian appetizer in the fall, direct from our family's garden and then stored in Ball canning jars ahead of the frost. Try serving them like you would a pickle on homemade deli meat sandwiches. Serve with other appetizers like olives and lupine beans. Or, put a bow on them and give as birthday or Christmas presents.

GARBANZO BEAN DIP ✠
(Hummus)

Bro. Joseph

- 2 cans garbanzo beans
- 1 lemon juiced
- 4 cloves garlic
- 4 tablespoons Tahini paste (optional)
- 1 teaspoon sea salt
- 1 teaspoon cumin (optional)
- ½ cup minced fresh parsley
- ¼ cup olive oil

First, drain beans and retain the water in a cup. Place in a food processor or blender with lemon juice, garlic, Tahini paste, sea salt, and cumin. Pulse mixture, occasionally adding the retained bean water to form a smooth thick paste. Be careful not to over water. Place dip in a small- to medium-sized bowl. Sprinkle with ¼ cup olive oil and confetti of fresh minced parsley. Serve with a platter of pita bread, cut into wedges and warmed in the oven for 10 minutes at 400 degrees F. You can also garnish the dip with a platter of fresh vegetables. Serve the dip freshly made or prepare a day early, cover, and refrigerate. The dip should be removed from the refrigerator 15 minutes before serving.

Note: From archaeological digs, we know people have eaten hummus (chickpeas) in the Middle East for more than 10,000 years. That predates writing! The tahini part of hummus is made from sesame seeds and also has been consumed in the Middle East since thousands of years B.C..

HOMEMADE COUGH SYRUP ★
(Sciroppo di Italiano)

Paula Grappo
Serves 1 Person

- 3 oz. Jim Beam, Seagram's 7 or Jack Daniels
- 3 oz. fresh squeezed lemon juice (lemon concentrate optional)
- 3 oz. raw clover or orange honey
- 3 oz. water (optional)

Place all ingredients in a Ball pint jar with secure lid. Shake until the honey is dissolved and forms into a syrupy mix. Take one to two tablespoons full every few hours. Cover and place in a medicine cabinet. Keep out of reach of children.

Note: Paula saved the day and gave this to us kids as a last-minute remedy when a cough was keeping the family up all night. It works like a charm to quiet a cough and help everyone get some rest. If the cough persisted after a day or so, it would be time for Dr. Middleton to come over (he made house calls) and prescribe some grape cough syrup with codeine!

HOMEMADE YOGURT ♥
(Yaourt à la Maison)

Bro. Joseph
Serves 4

½ gallon organic whole milk
2 heaping tablespoons of plain yogurt

In a large nonstick sauce pan, heat milk to a low simmer, stirring frequently. Remove and set pot on a cooling rack. Wash hands and place finger in milk after one hour to test for lukewarmness. Once it is lukewarm, whisk 2 heaping tablespoons of plain yogurt into the pot. Cover the top with cellophane and wrap completely in a small blanket, setting on the counter in a warm spot for four hours. Next, place in the refrigerator overnight with 1 or 2 clean dishtowels on top of the yogurt to remove excess liquid. Ring out and replace towels until desired thickness is achieved. Serve the next day with honey and/or fresh fruit and granola.

Note: Most historical accounts attribute yogurt to the Neolithic peoples of Central Asia around 6000 B.C.. Herdsmen began the practice of milking their animals, and then carrying the containers home, discovering yogurt when they arrived.

ITALIAN OLIVES 🌐
(Italian Oil Cured Dried Black Olives)

Paula Grappo
Serves 4 - 6

1 bottle (10 oz.) Italian-style oil cured black olives (available at Amazon.com, Italian grocers and Walmart online)
Olive oil
Red pepper flakes
1 teaspoon garlic minced
Pinch of dried oregano and basil

Add all ingredients in a medium-sized mixing bowl. Toss with a spoon, along with a splash or two of olive oil. Pack the olives into a bottle or a pint-sized canning jar and refrigerate. Serve plain as an appetizer or as part of an antipasto plate, including lupini beans, provolone, mozzarella, crackers, Italian bread, green olives, and stuffed celery.

Note: The harvesting of olives is almost always done by hand - slow, labor-intensive work, usually done without mechanical devices of any kind except maybe a rake. Olives are easily bruised and must be handled gently, especially "table olives," meaning those intended to be eaten as antipasto. Most olives we eat are from Italy, Greece, France, Spain, Portugal, and California.

LUPINI BEANS 🌎
(Fagioli Lupini)

Elizabeth Catanzarite
Serves 12 - 24 Appetizer-style

1.5 to 2 lbs. dried lupini beans   Sea salt
(available at Amazon.com)

On day one, rinse the beans and heat them on simmer, in a generous amount of water, for about an hour. Then, run the beans under cold water. From there, put them in a glass jar, a crock pot, or a stainless steel pot with a lot of fresh water and a small palm of salt. Cover and set in a corner at room temperature. Every day for 10 days rinse the beans, fill with fresh water and a small palm of salt. On the tenth day, rinse the beans, transfer portions to Ball pint jars (about four to five jars), add fresh water and one to two teaspoons of salt. Then, refrigerate. They will keep for months in the refrigerator—until all are eaten. If the water gets cloudy over time, dump it, rinse the beans, and add fresh water and salt to taste. If the beans are too salty for any reason, rinse them, add fresh water, and reduce the amount of salt that you put in last time. Serve cold before dinner as an appetizer or eat at night for a low-carb, high-fiber, healthy snack. Lupini beans can be eaten with skins on or pop the skins off one by one and just eat the beans. The ten-day method is an ancient Roman recipe which must be followed. Otherwise the beans taste very bitter and are poisonous to eat in large quantities. Also, each day while rinsing, as they surface in the water, be sure to "weed" out beans that have brown spots, other discoloration, or those that break apart from their shells. When preparing to bottle and serve, you will have a more consistent and appealing appetizer for your family and guests. My grandmother, Elizabeth, made lupini beans special for Thanksgiving, Christmastime, and Easter.

Note: Historically, lupini beans have been cultivated as far back as the Egyptian empire 2,000 BCE. Afterwards, the Greek and Roman Empires' street vendors marketed them across the Mediterranean region—along with a glass of beer or wine. They are high in bitter, toxic flavors that—with proper preparation—can be washed out in about 10 days. They are high in protein.

OLIVE APPETIZER ✠
(Antipasto di Oliva)

Bro. Joseph

30-oz. jar Kalamata pitted olives
20-oz. jar Queen Ann Spanish Pimento Stuffed Olives
¼ cup olive oil
6 garlic cloves fresh minced
1 tablespoon red pepper flakes
1 tablespoon oregano

Drain olives. Place drained olives in a mixing bowl with olive oil, minced garlic, red pepper flakes, and oregano. Mix gently, but thoroughly. Store in refrigerator in pint or quart-sized Ball canning jars. Remove 10 minutes before serving. Garnish with slices of provolone, mozzarella and Carr's water crackers. This appetizer pairs well with a glass of Chardonnay or Chianti.

Note: The olive was native to Iran, Syria, and Palestine and spread to the rest of the Mediterranean basin 6,000 years ago. Olive trees are among the oldest-known, cultivated trees in the world—being grown before the written language was invented.

ORANGE LEMONADE
(Fresh Homemade Orange Lemonade)

Bro. Joseph
Serves 8 - 10
Refreshing Summer Cooler

- 2 cups sugar
- 2 cups water
- 1 cup fresh-squeezed lemon juice
- 1 cup fresh-squeezed orange juice
- 1 lemon thinly-sliced, with rind, remove seeds
- 1 orange thinly sliced, with rind, remove seeds
- 6 cups of cold water
- 1 gallon Rubbermaid pitcher
- 2 trays of ice cubes

Boil two cups of water. Turn off the heat and stir in the sugar until melted, forming a clear syrup. Add the syrup to the Rubbermaid one-gallon pitcher, along with six cups of cold water. Then add the fresh-squeezed orange and lemon juice. Stir vigorously. After stirring, add the lemon and orange slices and stir again. Store in the refrigerator overnight for more chill and a tasty blend of flavors or serve fresh right away over ice. For large family gatherings, feel free to augment the recipe with additions, such as a few tablespoons of Tang and a few tablespoons of Real Lemon Juice from the bottle. Then add sugar, water, and ice to taste.

Note: This is a family favorite for summer picnics, barbecues, or just for a healthy and refreshing drink to keep everyone hydrated during the hot days of the season. It's a great product for the children's lemonade stand!

ROASTED RED PEPPERS ★
(Peperoni Arrosto)

Paula Grappo
Makes two pint jars

2 dozen fresh red bell peppers, washed and dried
4 tablespoons garlic minced
Red pepper flakes
Dried oregano
Dried basil
Sea salt
Olive oil

On a foil-lined cookie sheet, roast the red bell peppers under the oven's broiler until burned on all sides. Remove from the oven and place the peppers in a large paper bag for five minutes. Peel, core, and slice the meat of the peppers into strips. In a large mixing bowl, toss the peppers with minced garlic, red pepper flakes, oregano, basil, sea salt, and olive oil. Pack into pint jars and refrigerate. Use on sandwiches, crackers, cheese slices, snacks, or a garnish for bruschetta, meats, and salads.

Note: Paula usually made these in the fall, before the last frost. Over the winter, they store best packed in pint jars in the refrigerator. We also baked them on top of homemade pizzas, or as part of an antipasto platter with stuffed celery, olives, and lupini beans.

SHRIMP COCKTAIL ✜
(Shrimp with Homemade Cocktail Sauce)

Bro. Joseph

1 to 2 lbs. shrimp, cooked, peeled, prepared, and chilled
½ cup Heinz Chili Sauce, plus ½ cup tomato ketchup
2 (or more) teaspoons of your favorite horseradish
2 or 3 grinds of fresh black pepper (optional)

Combine tomato ketchup and horseradish to taste. Place in a small dip bowl, in the center of a platter. Line the platter with crisp, cold, dry leaves of lettuce. Place shrimp on the platter around the shrimp cocktail sauce bowl. Feel free to add color by garnishing the bowl and shrimp platter with sprigs of parsley.

Note: From housewives entertaining husbands' bosses, to family weddings and restaurant outings, shrimp cocktail was the most popular hors d'oeuvre in Great Britain and the United States from the 1960s to the late 1980s. It is still loved by many today.

STUFFED DATES ⊗
(Dates Wrapped with Bacon Appetizer)

Bro. Joseph

8 slices of bacon cut in half
16 pitted dates
32 almond slivers

4 oz goat or blue cheese
Toothpicks

Preheat the oven to 350 degrees F. Using your fingers, stuff two almond slivers or a small amount of goat or blue cheese into the cavity of each date. Cut the bacon slices in half. Wrap each date with a slice of bacon and secure with a toothpick. Arrange evenly on a baking sheet with raised edges (otherwise grease will spread) and bake for 10 minutes. Remove the dates and use the toothpick to turn each one so it's laying on its side. Bake for another five to eight minutes, until browned to your liking. Turn the dates to the other side and repeat. Remove from the oven, place on a paper towel-lined plate, and let stand for five minutes before serving.

Note: An Arabic legend tells of the date palm's creation: "After God had finished molding Man from Earth; He took the remaining material and shaped it into a date palm which he placed in the Garden of Eden." Before the existence of Man, over 50,000 years ago, date palms evolved to being instrumental to early humans' lives in the Mid-east and now cultivated in California as well.

STUFFED MUSHROOMS ⊗

Angela Chavez
Serves 6 - 8

1 pack fresh mushrooms, dusted with a paper towel and stems removed

1 8-oz pack Philadelphia Cream Cheese
1 roll of Jimmy Dean Sausage

Cook sausage, drain, and place in a medium mixing bowl. Gently combine with the cream cheese. (Optional is to add a teaspoon of minced fresh onion and two tablespoons of bread crumbs.) With a teaspoon, stuff each mushroom with the mixture and place on an ungreased cookie sheet. Bake at 350 F for 20 minutes. Serve hot. Enjoy!

Note: Stuffed mushrooms are a party favorite and Angela has been making them for her family and friends for decades!

SWEET AND SOUR MEATBALLS ★
(Pineapple Glazed Meatballs)

Bro. Joseph
Serves 6 - 10

- 1 bag (25 pieces) frozen meatballs or. . .
- 1 recipe homemade Italian meatballs (omit Italian Parmesan cheese)
- ½ cup brown sugar
- ½ cup white vinegar
- ¼ cup ketchup
- 1 tablespoon hot sauce
- 2 cans pineapple chunks, drained
- Juice from 2 cans of pineapple chunks, with water to form 2 cups liquid
- 1 tablespoon cornstarch
- 1 recipe of Jasmine or Basmati rice
- ½ cup green onions sliced for garnish
- Sesame seeds (optional garnish)

If rolling your own meatballs, make them smaller than you would for spaghetti sauce. Spread the meatballs in a baking dish using non-stick cooking spray, and bake for 20 to 25 minutes at 350 F. While they are baking, make the sauce. In a medium-sized sauce pan, combine the brown sugar, white vinegar, ketchup, hot sauce, pineapple liquid, and a heaping tablespoon of cornstarch. Simmer on low until it thickens. Fold in pineapple chunks and pour over baked meatballs. Simmer in the oven at 350—uncovered—for 30 minutes. Serve with rice or as an appetizer with toothpicks. Garnish with sliced green onions and/or sesame seeds.

Note: The meatballs may be rolled and frozen on cookie trays ahead of time. Once frozen, store in one quart slider bags to save room in the freezer.

WATERMELON FETA CHEESE APPETIZER ⊘
(Watermelon Poppers)

Bro. Joseph
Serves 8 - 10

1 small watermelon peeled, seeded, and cut into bite-size squares
16 oz. Feta cheese cut into small bits
1 large bunch fresh mint, washed and dried
1 pack party toothpicks

Place watermelon squares on paper towels. Assemble each square with a toothpick, mint leaf, and small amount of Feta cheese. Arrange on an appetizer plate, tightly wrap with cellophane, and chill until ready to serve. Can be made a few hours ahead of time, but not overnight or the mint leaves may wilt. For a change, try using fresh basil instead of mint. Also, try adding slivers of red onion and cracked black pepper for more spice.

Note: Feta cheese watermelon poppers are an addicting, 20-minute, gluten-free appetizer recipe. Perfect for parties, summer patio dinners, and barbecues!

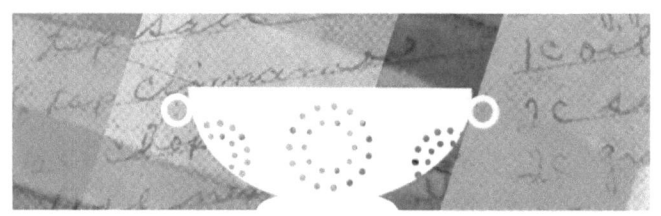

Soups & Salads

SOUPS & SALADS

BEEF VEGETABLE SOUP ❄
(Old Fashion Beef Stew)

Bro. Joseph
Serves 4 - 6

- 3 lbs. beef chuck or round roast, cut into cubes
- 1 medium onion chopped
- ¾ cup flour
- 2 to 3 cups beef bouillon, made according to package directions
- 1 cup of Masala, Merlot or Cabernet Sauvignon
- 3 stalks celery chopped
- 5 medium carrots washed, peeled, and sliced
- 2 tablespoons fresh or dried thyme minced
- 2 cloves garlic crushed
- 2 bay leaves
- Pepper to taste

Wash and pat dry beef chunks. Dredge in the flour until well covered. Sauté and brown the meat using a large nonstick frying pan with 2 tablespoons of oil and two tablespoons of melted butter. Place the browned meat in a large soup pot with all other ingredients. Simmer on low for 2 to 3 hours until meat is tender. Serve with your favorite Italian bread, French bread, pizza slice, or cornbread.

Note: The rain, sleet, or snow is swirling about on a dreary winter's day. It's the perfect reason to stay indoors and make a pot of hearty old-fashioned beef stew and homemade bread!

BEET SALAD ♥
(Salade de Betteraves d'Hiver)

Paula Grappo
Serves 4 - 6

2 cans of sliced or whole beets cut in half and well-drained
2 celery sticks thinly sliced
½ small onion minced
¼ cup fresh parsley minced (optional)
Oil and vinegar
Salt and fresh ground pepper to taste

In a small salad bowl, combine all the ingredients and toss 20 times to meld the flavors. Cover and place in the refrigerator for anywhere from one hour to overnight. Serve with your favorite Italian or French bread from the local bakery. Beet salad makes a great side dish for pasta dinners, as well as with oven-baked or pan-seared meats.

Note: Paula made this dish, usually in the winter, when lettuce prices soared in the markets. It's a great way to serve a nutritious and delicious salad—without the expense of ingredients that aren't in season, and would have to be imported from faraway lands. In old-world countries like Switzerland and France, beets are a staple during the wintertime to this very day.

BLACK BEAN CUBAN SALAD 🍎
(Ensalada de Frijol Negro Cubano)

Bro. Joseph
Serves 6 - 8

- 2 cans black beans washed and drained or cook 1 bag dried black beans tender, rinse and drain
- 1 can corn or ¼ bag frozen corn blanched in hot water, rinsed in cold water and drained
- ½ small onion minced
- 2 carrots washed, peeled, and minced
- 2 celery sticks washed and minced
- ¼ cup fresh cilantro minced
- 2 small tomatoes minced
- 1 cucumber peeled, seeded, and chopped
- 1 or 2 jalapeño peppers minced (optional)
- 1 red or yellow bell pepper chopped
- Olive oil and vinegar
- Salt and fresh ground pepper to taste
- 1 fresh lemon and lime—both juiced (optional)
- 1 teaspoon sugar (optional)
- 1 avocado chopped (optional)
- 1 tablespoon dried cumin powder

In a large salad bowl, toss all ingredients together with a salad fork and spoon—about 20 times to meld the flavors. Chill anywhere from 1 hour to overnight. Serve as a side dish with fresh French or Italian bread. Serve as a main dish, topped with a dab of sour cream or pieces of all white StarKist tuna or grilled chicken strips.

Note: Although Spain and Africa contributed most to Cuban cuisine, the French, Arabic, Chinese, and Portuguese cultures were also influential. Traditional Cuban dishes generally lack seasonings and sauces. Black beans, stews, and meats are the most popular foods. Root vegetables are often flavored with mojoa—a combination of olive oil, lemon juice, onions, garlic, and cumin.

CABBAGE AND WHITE BEAN SOUP ♥

Bro. Joseph
Serves 6 - 8

1 head cabbage chopped
6 to 8 cups water
4 tablespoons chicken bouillon
4 potatoes peeled and diced into chunks
4 carrots peeled and cut into thick slices
1 can white beans drained and washed
1 or 2 jalapeño peppers chopped
1 medium onion chopped
6 garlic cloves chopped
1 lb. ground turkey sautéed in a little oil and garlic salt
Fresh ground black pepper to taste
⅓ cup olive oil

In a large soup pan, heat the following on medium: chopped cabbage, chicken bouillon, carrots, potatoes, fried ground meat, white beans and 6 to 8 cups of water. In a large skillet, heat the following on medium-high: olive oil, garlic, onions, and jalapeño peppers (in their own section of the skillet). Try to keep them separate in the pan. Stir occasionally until lightly browned. Quickly scrape all into the soup. Add salt and pepper to taste. Simmer uncovered on low heat for 30 to 60 minutes. Stores well in quart jars and tastes even better when heated and served. It's a great meal when served with corn bread, homemade bread, or pizza.

Note: Paula made this quite often during the winter months and usually served it on weeknights, with homemade bread or pizza for family dinners. In the winter we would also have a beet or green tomato salad. Adding the jalapeño pepper is my creation (California-Mexican influence), as well as adding the ground turkey.

DANDELION SALAD ♥
(Spring Greens Salad)

Jim Grappo, Sr.
4 - 6

1 large bowl of freshly-picked early spring dandelion greens from the country, from a chemical free pasture

Wine vinegar
Olive oil
Sea salt or garlic salt
1 small onion minced

In the early spring, pick dandelion field greens, using a knife to cut under the center at the root. Be sure to pick from fields that are free of pesticides and foot traffic. At home, using a small paring knife, trim off some of the bottom root and yellowed leaves. Then, triple wash in a lot of cold water. Next, shake and pat dry with paper towels. At this point, you can store in one-gallon slider bags, or cut them up and place the greens in a large salad bowl. Chill in the refrigerator for about 30 minutes. When ready, dress the salad with minced onion, wine vinegar, olive oil and salt to taste. Serve fresh with pasta, pizza, or your favorite Italian or French bread. (Be sure to ask the farm owner first, but most will gladly let you pick dandelions from their un-planted fields. Also, look around creeks, brooks, and rivers. They grow in abundance next to wet locations in the early spring.

Note: Served raw in a salad, dandelion greens pack a punch with healthy fiber, iron, minerals, vitamin C and more! Also, dandelion greens may be grown in your garden and harvested before the yellow flower forms. After flowers form, the greens become too bitter. Dandelions may be picked, washed, and blanched for a minute in boiling water. Freeze and use throughout the year.

ITALIAN BREAD BEAN SOUP 🍎
(Pancotto)

Bro. Joseph

½ lb. stale Italian or French bread, set out overnight to harden
⅛ cup olive oil
1 small onion minced
1 clove garlic minced
1 teaspoon sea salt or chicken bouillon
4 cups water
½ cup basil, chives, or parsley minced
2 to 4 grinds fresh pepper
1 can white or cannellini beans washed and drained

Break bread up or cut into one inch cubes. Set aside. In a large sauce pot, sauté onion and garlic in olive oil until light brown. Quickly add bread and water to form a thick soup. Add one small can of well-rinsed white navy beans or white cannellini beans. Stir and warm. Serve with Parmesan cheese, extra drizzle of olive oil per dish, a few grinds of pepper, and fresh minced herbs like basil, parsley, or chives. Also, many Italians enjoy a thin slice of fresh white onion with this dish. Leftovers store well and can be reheated the next day by adding a little extra water.

Note: For hundreds of years, Pancotto has been a simple, comforting peasant dish that spans almost every region in Italy. It is also an Italian tradition to serve bread soup on meatless days during Lent. Families love it!

LENTIL SOUP 🕊
(Cappadocia-style Lentil Soup)

Bro. Joseph
Serves 4 - 6

1 bag lentils washed, remove debris, stones, and cook according to package directions
1 large potato washed, peeled, and cubed
1 large carrot washed, peeled, and cubed
1 onion chopped finely
¼ cup olive oil

2 teaspoons powdered cumin
2 tablespoons sesame seeds (optional)
1 teaspoon nutmeg
Sea salt and fresh ground pepper to taste
1 stock of celery chopped
1 fresh lemon, seeds removed and juiced

Sauté the following in a large nonstick frying pan on medium-high heat: chopped potato, onion, carrot, and celery in olive oil. Combine the cooked lentils, cumin, nutmeg, and juice of one lemon into the nonstick frying pan. Simmer on low for 10 minutes to bring the flavors together. Serve hot with fresh Italian or French bread and before serving top each guest's serving bowl with drizzles of olive oil and sprinkles of sesame seeds.

Note: Cappadocia is a desert region in central Turkey, known for its tall, cone-shaped rock formations and caves near Göreme and elsewhere. Early Christian cave dwellers used the region as a refuge from persecution. Lentils have been cultivated for thousands of years in Cappadocia and are a staple to this very day. Lentils are served year-round, but especially during Lent.

PARSLEY SALAD OF LEBANON 🌐
(Tabbouleh)

Mary Catanzarite
6 appetizer servings
4 dinner salad servings

- ¼ cup fine bulgur wheat soaked in a bowl with a slight covering of water for 20 minutes
- 1 garlic clove minced
- 2 large lemons, juiced and strained
- 3 cups fresh parsley, washed, leafy, chopped
- ¼ cup fresh mint, washed and chopped
- 1 small bunch green onions, washed and thinly sliced
- 4 small- or medium-sized tomatoes chopped
- ¼ cup extra virgin olive oil
- Sea salt and fresh ground pepper to taste

Drain and press the water out of the bulgur by using a medium-sized kitchen strainer. Place in a large salad bowl, and toss with the garlic, lemon juice, parsley, mint, tomatoes, green onions, and salt. Place in the refrigerator for two to three hours so that the bulgur continues to absorb liquid, swell, and have its flavors meld together. This dish can be made one day ahead of time.

Note: Aunt Mary, an amazing chef from the old-country (Paula's sister-in-law married to Pat, her brother) was from Lebanon and introduced our Italian family to many culinary favorites. Also, as a teenager, I was the lawn keeper for "Our Lady of Lebanon National Shrine" and was introduced to hummus, homemade yogurt, kibi and other recipes the priests and nuns brought to America!

PASTA AND BEANS SOUP ♣
(Zuppa di Pasta e Fagioli)

Paula Grappo

- 1 box pasta shells, elbows, or box of spaghetti broken into thirds
- 8 cups chicken bouillon broth
- 1 small onion minced
- 4 cloves garlic minced
- 1 can white beans, cannelloni beans, or chickpeas rinsed and drained
- ¼ cup olive oil
- 2 stalks of celery minced
- 2 carrots minced
- 2 tablespoons fresh rosemary minced or 1 tablespoon dried oregano
- 2 teaspoons fresh ground pepper
- 1 large can tomatoes crushed or cut
- 1 cup minced ham, pancetta or minced crispy bacon (optional)

Make pasta according to package directions "Al Dente." Set aside in cold water to stop cooking and drain well. Next, in a large soup pan, sauté all the minced vegetables in olive oil to a light golden brown. Now, add the 8 cups of broth to the pan, along with beans, pasta, tomatoes, minced meat, ground pepper and rosemary or oregano. Bring to a simmer and ladle soup into 8 oz pasta bowls or individual soup bowls. For a lighter, looser soup, serve shortly after combining ingredients. For a thicker soup, simmer longer—until the pasta absorbs more of the liquid. If it gets too thick just add water and/or a small can of Hunts Sauce. Serve with a garnish of fresh basil confetti or chopped fresh rosemary—along with Italian Parmesan cheese and red pepper flakes. A drizzle of olive oil and fresh ground black pepper over the top of each dish goes well too. (For a creative twist that children love, try making the recipe with one can of Campbell's Pork 'n Beans, instead of white beans.)

Note: This is old-world, peasant comfort food at its best. Serve on a cold winter's night with a glass of white wine or red Italian Chianti—along with some homemade Italian bread, rolls, pizza or rosemary foccacia flat bread. Pasta e Fagioli is also a popular meatless Lenten dish among Italians. The soup is filling and outstanding without the meat.

PEAR SALAD FOR FALL
(Salad de poires pour l'automne)

Bro. Joseph
Serves 4

1 recipe raspberry sauce (see desserts)
1 head bib lettuce washed and dried or 1 bag spring mix
2 pears, cored and sliced
4 oz. Feta cheese
1 small red onion sliced thinly
1 cup lightly chopped pecans
Sea salt and fresh ground pepper to taste
1 small pack fresh raspberries
Lemon juice fresh or bottled

Divide lettuce evenly across four salad bowls. Dip pear slices in lemon juice and arrange evenly across four bowls. Divide red onion slices, one ounce of Feta cheese and pecans evenly across four salad bowls. Right before serving, pour cold raspberry sauce over each or cold raspberry vinaigrette. Garnish each plate with fresh raspberries. Lightly sprinkle sea salt and fresh ground pepper to taste.

Note: Serve with roasted turkey breast and stuffing. Also, this salad goes well with pan-seared fillet mignon, deglazed with red wine/butter and served au jus with scalloped potatoes. If pear salad is prepared ahead of time, then seal each one with Glad Wrap and store in the refrigerator. Add raspberry sauce or dressing right before serving.

SALAD WITH TUNA ♥
(Salade Américaine Nicoise)

Bro. Joseph
Serves 4 - 6

1 head iceberg, bib, red or endive lettuce washed, dried, and chopped
1 small onion finely chopped or ½ cup sliced green onions
2 carrots washed, peeled and finely chopped or shredded
2 celery sticks, washed and thinly sliced
1 can black olives drained
1 large can all-white tuna drained well

4 tablespoons of fresh herbs chopped finely - cilantro, basil or thyme
2 medium-sized tomatoes chopped
Olive oil and red wine vinegar
Sea salt and fresh ground pepper
1 large handful fresh green beans, blanched and chilled (optional)

In a mixing bowl or large meat platter, lay out lettuce. Alternate sprinkles of onion, olives, tomatoes, celery, carrots, green beans, and herbs until all are used up. Top the salad with shreds of white tuna. Right before serving, sprinkle salad with red wine vinegar, olive oil, sea salt, and fresh ground pepper. Serve with fresh French or Italian bread, focaccia flat bread, Carr's Water Crackers or homemade cornbread.

Note: This salad is a meal in itself! Works well any day of the week, as well as for meatless days during Lent. The recipe is American-style, but patterned after Salade Nicoise, a French country favorite. Hint: substitute 1 small tub of cottage cheese or 1 well-drained can of corn for the tuna as a wonderful vegetarian variation.

SUISSE CARROT SALAD
(Salade Suisse de Carottes)

Bro. Joseph
Serves 6 - 8

1 small bag fresh carrots washed, peeled, trimmed, and shredded
2 small containers of plain yogurt
1 tablespoon sugar
1 tablespoon French or American mustard
2 teaspoons fresh garlic mashed (pulverized)
Sea salt and fresh ground pepper to taste

Combine all ingredients in a mixing bowl and stir 25 to 50 times. Add salt and pepper to taste. Chill for at least one hour or overnight before serving.

Note: The Swiss call this "root" salad and they mainly prepare it in the winter when fresh produce is out of season in local gardens in the Swiss Alps. Try substituting the carrots for other types of roots, shred and toss with the same ingredients as above. Try washing, peeling, and shredding turnips, parsnips, or celeriac root—all of which are available in the winter months.

TOMATO SALAD
(Summer Garden Italian Tomato Salad)

Paula Grappo
Serves 4 - 6

4 fresh medium- to large-sized red, juicy tomatoes
1 small onion, cut into thin slices
1 bell pepper, cut into thin slices and then cut in half
¼ cup olive oil
⅓ cup very cold water
1 teaspoon oregano
Garlic salt and fresh ground pepper to taste
¼ cup fresh basil chopped (optional)
½ lb. fresh Italian Mozzarella cheese, cut and cubed (optional)
1 clove garlic finely minced (optional)

Place all ingredients in a medium-sized salad bowl and gently toss 20 times to meld the flavors. Set in refrigerator for one hour before serving. By following the optional ingredients, you can make this recipe as basic (peasant food) or as "a la Roma" chic as you wish.

Note: In the years after the war (1945), families did not have a lot of choices year-round like we do today. Seasonal cooking was a must. In the summer, when gardens were in full bloom, a fresh-made Italian tomato salad was served frequently, with a lot of fresh Italian bread for dipping in the juice, thus the ⅓ cup of cold water!

WINTER TOMATO SALAD 🌎
(Pickled Green Tomato Salad)

Paula Grappo

1 Ohio Stoneware 5-gallon crock (Available at Ace Hardware)
15 to 20 green tomatoes of all shapes and sizes
2 gallons apple cider vinegar
1 handful sea salt
1 gallon of water

In September or October, pick the green tomatoes before the first frost. Wash, remove stems and leaves, and place all ingredients in the crock. Stir with a large soup spoon. Cover with a stoneware dish and top off with a sealed Ball quart jar—filled with water to sink the tomatoes below the vinegar line. Let it stand in a cool corner or basement for 60 days. If you live in a warm climate, you can put the tomatoes up in three or four large kitchen jars (WalMart) and pickle on the bottom shelf of the refrigerator for two months. After two months, slice the tomatoes into a large salad bowl. Add olive oil, sea salt, dried oregano, chopped garlic, and red pepper flakes. Stir very well. Put up in quart or pint canning jars and place in the refrigerator for many winter salads and sandwich garnishes, or gift as Christmas presents. Before serving, take out of the refrigerator and let stand at room temperature for 10 minutes allowing the olive oil to melt and blend with the tomatoes.

Note: For hundreds of years, pickling green tomatoes for the winter has been popular among Polish, Italian, Jewish, and many Germanic cultures. Paula served green tomato salad as a way to serve up flavor and lower the cost of buying expensive fresh produce shipped in from other countries during the wintertime.

WINTER TOMATO SALAD 🌎
(Pickled Green Tomato Salad)

Paula Grappo

1 Ohio Stoneware 5-gallon crock (Available at Ace Hardware)
15 to 20 green tomatoes of all shapes and sizes
2 gallons apple cider vinegar
1 handful sea salt
1 gallon of water

In September or October, pick the green tomatoes before the first frost. Wash, remove stems and leaves, and place all ingredients in the crock. Stir with a large soup spoon. Cover with a stoneware dish and top off with a sealed Ball quart jar—filled with water to sink the tomatoes below the vinegar line. Let it stand in a cool corner or basement for 60 days. If you live in a warm climate, you can put the tomatoes up in three or four large kitchen jars (WalMart) and pickle on the bottom shelf of the refrigerator for two months. After two months, slice the tomatoes into a large salad bowl. Add olive oil, sea salt, dried oregano, chopped garlic, and red pepper flakes. Stir very well. Put up in quart or pint canning jars and place in the refrigerator for many winter salads and sandwich garnishes, or gift as Christmas presents. Before serving, take out of the refrigerator and let stand at room temperature for 10 minutes allowing the olive oil to melt and blend with the tomatoes.

Note: For hundreds of years, pickling green tomatoes for the winter has been popular among Polish, Italian, Jewish, and many Germanic cultures. Paula served green tomato salad as a way to serve up flavor and lower the cost of buying expensive fresh produce shipped in from other countries during the wintertime.

Vegetables & Side Dishes

VEGETABLES & SIDE DISHES

APPLE CHUTNEY ★
(Apple Sauce)

Bro. Joseph
4 - 6

- 4 medium- to large-sized baking apples, peeled, cored, and chopped into chunks
- ½ cup brown sugar or for diabetics ¼ cup Splenda Brown Sugar Blend
- 1 tablespoon butter
- 1 tablespoon lemon juice
- 1 teaspoon cinnamon
- 1 pinch each allspice, cloves, nutmeg, and pumpkin spice (optional)
- ¼ cup raisins (or more as you like)
- 1 tablespoon water

Place all of the ingredients (except raisins) into a medium-sized sauce pan and bring to a simmer. Keep heat low and cook—covered—for 20 minutes. Now, using a fork or potato masher, smash the apples into a chunky apple sauce. Then, add the raisins and simmer on low until reduced into a thick chutney. Serve as a side to roasted pork loin or pork chops. Or, prepare as a warm topping for a big scoop of Ben & Jerry's vanilla ice cream or apple cake.

Note: The original chutney of India (Hindi: chatni) was usually a relish made from fresh fruits and spices. They range in flavor from sweet or sour, spicy or mild, or any combination of these. They can be thin or chunky and can be made with fruits, vegetables, or both.

BEANS AND GREENS ♥
(Manestra)

Bro. Joseph
Serves 4

- 1 can of cannellini beans or Great Northern white beans, washed and drained
- 7 cloves garlic, peeled and minced
- 1 sprig of fresh rosemary or one tablespoon crushed rosemary
- 3 handfuls of triple washed greens, swiss chard, spinach, collards, escarole, or endive
- 1 shallot or 1 small white onion minced
- 3 tablespoons of red wine vinegar
- ¼ cup extra virgin olive oil
- Sea salt and fresh ground pepper to taste
- 1 teaspoon chicken bouillon

Place beans in a large skillet with one cup of water and one teaspoon of chicken bouillon. Add rosemary and bring to a low simmer. In a small frying pan, sauté the shallot or white onion along with the minced garlic in olive oil until light golden brown. Pour into beans. Add handfuls of greens, red wine vinegar and wilt over low heat. Simmer and reduce heat for one to two minutes. Serve hot with Italian or French bread. Excellent side dish for serving with braised, grilled, or baked meats and poultry.

Note: Maneštra (from Italian minestra, "soup") is a bean and vegetable stew —made especially in the springtime—with field greens. It is popular in the whole of the northern Adriatic Sea, Italy and surrounding countries. Feeling creative? Add fresh plum tomatoes, chopped, or a small can of whole-crushed tomatoes for a tasty change.

CABBAGE AND POTATOES
(Polish Cabbage and Smashed Potatoes)

Paula Grappo
Serves 4 - 6

1 medium-sized head of cabbage chopped
1 large onion chopped
4 large Russet potatoes, washed, peeled, chopped, and boiled tender
¼ cup canola or olive oil
Sea salt and fresh ground pepper to taste

In a very large skillet on medium-high heat, add oil, onion, and cabbage. Fry until lightly browned. Next, drain the potatoes well and add them to the skillet. Use a large fork or potato masher to smash and incorporate the cabbage, potatoes, and onions into one mixture. Add salt and ground pepper as needed. Place in a covered baking dish and keep in oven on low until you are ready to serve.

Note: A popular peasant dish in Eastern Europe, but packed with flavor! This is a hearty side dish for fish, other seafood, and meats. Paula made this dish popular among neighbors and friends—usually during the Lenten season on Fridays, as a side dish to accompany baked white fish or a fish fry.

CANDIED YAMS
(Thanksgiving and Christmas Yams)

Paula Grappo
Serves 6 - 8

2-3 pounds yams, boiled (not too soft), cooled, and peeled
½ cup brown sugar
½ stick of butter
¼ cup orange juice
½ teaspoon salt

When possible prepare the yams the night before to give them time to cool and become firm after boiling. Peel and cut into quarters. Set aside. In a large frying pan melt butter, brown sugar, orange juice, and salt together—on medium heat. Lay in the yams and simmer a few minutes until liquid thickens to a syrup. Spoon lightly over yams for better coating of the glaze. Serve hot.

Note: Without a doubt, by 1880 Americans were enjoying variations of candied sweet potatoes. American cookbooks, such as the widely published 1893 Boston Cooking School Cookbook by Fannie Farmer, featured a recipe for glazed sweet potatoes. However, historical facts point to evidence that for more than 200 years candied yams have been an American staple and tradition!

CHINESE FRIED RICE 🌏
(Yeung Chow Fried Rice)

Vern Seto
Serves 6 - 8

- 2 eggs (first time) scramble and pour paper thin in a greased large skillet
- 2 eggs (second time) scramble and pour paper thin in a greased large skillet
- 2 cups Jasmine or Basmati rice, cooked according to directions
- ¼ to ⅛ cup canola oil
- 1 small bag frozen BirdsEye peas and carrots
- Shredded pork and/or frozen cooked shrimp (optional)
- ½ cup green onions sliced
- 1 bottle soy sauce as needed

First, cook the two sets of two eggs as you would a crepe, very thin. Remove eggs from skillet and slice into thin strips. Place the rice in a very large nonstick skillet with canola oil. Fry on medium-high heat adding drizzles of soy sauce, then add the sliced eggs, and then the frozen peas and carrots. Now, add the sliced green onion and the sliced pork and/or shrimp. Simmer on medium heat—turning frequently for 20 minutes. Use a little extra oil, soy, and/or drops of water if it gets too dry.

Note: The exact origins of fried rice are lost to history. It's believed to have been invented sometime during the Sui dynasty (589-618 AD), in the city of Yangzhou in eastern Jiangsu province. Today, fried rice dishes are found throughout China, particularly in the south, where rice is the staple grain. This recipe has been in Vern's family since the 1900s.

CORN CASSEROLE
(Bisquick Corn Casserole)

Bro. Joseph

1 can whole kernel yellow corn drained
1 can cream-style yellow corn
1 8 oz. carton sour cream or cream cheese
2 eggs lightly beaten
2 cups Bisquick
½ stick melted butter
1 tablespoon sugar
1.5 cups bacon bits (optional)
½ cup shredded cheddar cheese

Preheat oven to 350 degrees. Use non-stick cooking spray on a 9" x 13" glass baking dish. In a large bowl, mix all ingredients together and pour into casserole dish. Bake at 350°F for 55 to 60 minutes. Sprinkle cheddar cheese on top 10 minutes before removing from the oven.

Note: According to General Mills, Bisquick was invented in 1930, after a top sales executive, Carl Smith, met an innovative train dining car chef on a business trip. After complimenting the chef's delicious fresh biscuits, the chef shared how he used a premixed biscuit batter of flour, salt, and lard. The rest is history! Bisquick was introduced on grocery shelves in 1931.

CORN FRITTERS

Paula Grappo
Serves 4 - 6

2 cups of corn, fresh, frozen, or canned
1 teaspoon of salt
⅛ teaspoon pepper
1 egg lightly scrambled
1 teaspoon melted butter
2 cups flour
2 teaspoons baking powder

Lightly chop corn with a knife on a cutting board or brief pulse in the food processor. In a large bowl, mix the corn with all ingredients except the flour and baking powder. Lastly, add the flour and baking powder by hand, stirring with a wooden spoon. The batter is similar to cookie batter. Drop by heaping teaspoon into hot oil, turning gently until golden brown on all sides. Remove and drain on paper towels. Serve hot with honey or maple syrup, along with baked or pan-fried fish.

Note: What kid doesn't like pancakes? These corn fritters make the sweet corn of summer merge with the maple pancake syrup of fall. That's when your children will love their vegetables for sure!

CORNMEAL FRIED 🍎
(Polenta Fritta)

Bro. Joseph

Yellow or white cornmeal, boiled   **1 heaping teaspoon of salt**
(to serve 4 to 6 people)

Slowly simmer cornmeal according to product instructions, and add salt to the water. Remove after cooking and pour into a 9" x 13" glass baking dish after using non-stick cooking spray or rubbing with oil. Chill four hours or overnight. Slice into squares like brownies. Fry each square in a nonstick skillet, with butter and a drop or two of oil. Brown each side on medium-high heat until crispy. Serve hot as a side dish with meats or a salad. Garnish with maple syrup on the side and serve with bacon and eggs—breakfast-style.

Note: For dinner, try serving slices of fried cornmeal with a topping of homemade spaghetti sauce, a meatball, and a sprinkle of Italian Parmesan cheese.

CRANBERRY CHUTNEY ★

Bro. Joseph
Serves 6 - 8

4 medium Granny Smith apples, washed, peeled, and cored
2 12-oz. bags fresh cranberries
2¼ cups sugar or 1.5 cups Truvia Sugar Blend
2 cups golden raisins (plumped in warm water)
½ cup orange juice
2 teaspoons grated orange peel
2 teaspoons salt
½ teaspoon allspice
2 15-oz. cans peaches, sliced and drained
2 15-oz. cans apricots, sliced and drained
2 cups pecans or walnuts, chopped (optional)

Combine all ingredients in a medium sauce pot—except peaches, apricots, and nuts. Simmer 10 minutes uncovered. Now add the rest of the ingredients and serve warm, or chill overnight and serve cold.

CRANBERRY RASPBERRY RELISH ⊗

Bro. Joseph
Serves 8 - 10

1 1-lb. bag fresh cranberries
2 Granny Smith apples, washed, peeled, and cored
1 cup sugar or ½ cup Truvia Sugar Blend
½ cup orange marmalade
1 10-oz. bag raspberries frozen
1 teaspoon lemon juice

Place cranberries and apples in a food processor. Chop to medium chop. Pour into a large mixing bowl, and add other ingredients. Gently stir with a wooden spoon until blended, about 25 to 50 stirs. Keeps for up to one month in the refrigerator.

Note: Try adding any one of the cranberry sauces as a spread on turkey or cold cut sandwiches—or as jam on fresh bread, butter, and toast.

CUCUMBER FREEZER PICKLES ❄

Bro. Joseph
Makes 4 - 6 Pint Canning Jars

2 quarts of pickle cucumbers, washed and sliced (Do not peel)
2 medium onions thinly sliced
1.5 cups sugar
½ cup white vinegar
¼ cup water

In a large mixing bowl, combine sliced cucumbers and onions. Toss, cover, and let rest for two hours. Next, in a saucepan bring the sugar, water and vinegar to a boil. Remove from stove and set aside. Drain all remaining liquid from vegetables. Now pack a mixture of cucumbers and onions into each jar. Lastly, pour syrup into each jar to about an inch below the top —to allow room for expansion. Freeze and take out as needed. Refrigerate any jars that go unused. They will keep for days for sandwiches and garnishes.

Note: Pickles have been around for thousands of years, dating back as far as 2030 BC—when cucumbers from native India were pickled in the Tigris Valley. In some traditions, pickled cucumbers are often fermented in saltwater brine. Cucumber pickles can also be made with a salt and vinegar brine.

FRESH CRANBERRY RELISH

Bro. Joseph
Serves 6 - 8

1 bag fresh cranberries washed
1 medium orange washed
2 apples, washed and cored

½ cup Splenda Brown Sugar Blend

In a food processor pulse cranberries until coarsely chopped. Pour them into a large mixing bowl. Next, quarter the orange and apples and place in food processor. Pulse until all is coarsely chopped. Pour into cranberries and toss 25 to 50 times with ½ cup Splenda Brown Sugar Blend. Let set one hour or overnight before transferring to a serving bowl. Excellent for Thanksgiving dinners, leftovers and Christmas parties—adding color and taste to the holiday season.

Note: Native Americans used the cranberries as a staple as early as 1550. By 1620 Pilgrims learned how to use cranberries from the Native Americans and soon incorporated the berries into American cuisine.

HOMINY
(Cherokee Indian Skillet Fried Hominy)

Bro. Joseph

1 28 oz. can hominy drained well
1 or 2 fresh jalapeño peppers minced
2 cloves garlic minced
1 small onion minced
½ stick butter and ⅛ cup vegetable oil

½ cup carrots minced and/or fresh tomato (optional)
1 can corn drained well (small- or medium-sized)
¼ cup fresh cilantro minced
1 teaspoon oregano
1 teaspoon garlic salt

Place butter and oil in nonstick skillet on medium-high heat. Once hot, sauté jalapeños, garlic, and onion until light brown. Add hominy, corn, and other ingredients, and brown lightly. Season to taste with garlic salt, a teaspoon of oregano, and minced cilantro. Serve immediately. Be creative—try adding bits of crispy bacon and/or shredded cheddar cheese over the top before serving. Hint: after draining the hominy and corn, line the bottom of a bowl with paper towels. Place both in the bowl to make the ingredients dry and easier to brown.

Note: Fried Hominy is a traditional Cherokee Native American Indian dish. Cherokee first settled in southeastern North America between A.D. 1000 and 1500.

FRESH CRANBERRY RELISH

Bro. Joseph
Serves 6 - 8

1 bag fresh cranberries washed
1 medium orange washed
2 apples, washed and cored
½ cup Splenda Brown Sugar Blend

In a food processor pulse cranberries until coarsely chopped. Pour them into a large mixing bowl. Next, quarter the orange and apples and place in food processor. Pulse until all is coarsely chopped. Pour into cranberries and toss 25 to 50 times with ½ cup Splenda Brown Sugar Blend. Let set one hour or overnight before transferring to a serving bowl. Excellent for Thanksgiving dinners, leftovers and Christmas parties—adding color and taste to the holiday season.

Note: Native Americans used the cranberries as a staple as early as 1550. By 1620 Pilgrims learned how to use cranberries from the Native Americans and soon incorporated the berries into American cuisine.

HOMINY
(Cherokee Indian Skillet Fried Hominy)

Bro. Joseph

1 28 oz. can hominy drained well
1 or 2 fresh jalapeño peppers minced
2 cloves garlic minced
1 small onion minced
½ stick butter and ⅛ cup vegetable oil

½ cup carrots minced and/or fresh tomato (optional)
1 can corn drained well (small- or medium-sized)
¼ cup fresh cilantro minced
1 teaspoon oregano
1 teaspoon garlic salt

Place butter and oil in nonstick skillet on medium-high heat. Once hot, sauté jalapeños, garlic, and onion until light brown. Add hominy, corn, and other ingredients, and brown lightly. Season to taste with garlic salt, a teaspoon of oregano, and minced cilantro. Serve immediately. Be creative—try adding bits of crispy bacon and/or shredded cheddar cheese over the top before serving. Hint: after draining the hominy and corn, line the bottom of a bowl with paper towels. Place both in the bowl to make the ingredients dry and easier to brown.

Note: Fried Hominy is a traditional Cherokee Native American Indian dish. Cherokee first settled in southeastern North America between A.D. 1000 and 1500.

MEXICAN FRIED RICE ⊗
(Arroz Frito Mexicano)

Coco Berberian
Serves 6 - 8

2 cups of Basmati or Jasmine rice uncooked
1 large can crushed tomatoes
5 cups vegetable or chicken bouillon broth (made according to directions)
1 small bag corn frozen
1 small bag peas
1 small onion minced
4 cloves garlic minced
Sea salt and pepper to taste
¼ cup canola oil

First, in a very large nonstick skillet add the canola oil, sprinkle the rice, and sauté until lightly browned—on medium-high heat. At the same time, sauté onion and garlic with the rice. Be careful not to burn the mixture. Next, add the crushed tomatoes, corn, peas, salt and pepper to taste, as well as the broth. Lastly, simmer on very low heat until the rice is tender (about 20 minutes), stirring frequently. If it gets too dry, add a little more water or broth. Optional: add pieces of shredded chicken or frozen baby shrimp during the time it simmers. Serve hot with tortilla chips, guacamole dip, a cold Corona with lime, and Maggie's chili bean recipe.

Note: In Mexico, this type of rice dish is referred to as "Arroz" which translates to "rice." If you order rice in northern Mexico, most likely you will get rice cooked with chicken broth and tomato flavors. In southern Mexico, plain white rice is more common. But—adding the broth, tomato, onion, and garlic is the Mexican way to add flavor to rice.

NOODLES AND CREAM CHEESE ⊛
(Polish Noodles)

Paula Grappo
Serves 4 - 6

1 large package of cream cheese
½ stick of butter
1 16 oz. package wide egg noodles or bow tie pasta
¼ cup milk

Make the noodles according to directions—Al Dente. Be careful not to overcook, slightly under cooking is better. Drain well and immediately place on low heat with butter and milk, as well as breaking the cream cheese into chunks. Gently fold and blend with a wooden spoon until warm and cheesy. Polish noodles go well with fish, seafood, and meats.

Note: Paula usually made this on Fridays with a fish dinner, especially during Lent. She learned the recipe from one of the Polish church ladies.

PEAS & PEARL ONIONS 🍎
(Petits Pois et Oignons au Beurre)

Bro. Joseph
Serves 4

1 small bag peas frozen
½ small bag pearl onions frozen
½ stick of butter

Garlic salt and ground pepper to taste
⅛ cup water

Combine all ingredients in a small sauce pan. Cover and bring to a simmer—then keep on low for three to five minutes. Serve hot.

Note: This is a perfect side dish to accompany a Sunday dinner of roast beef or herb-baked chicken.

PEAS AND EGGS 🍎

Paula Grappo
Serves 4

1 small bag peas frozen
½ small onion minced
1 egg whisked (with a fork in a cup)
½ stick of butter

1 teaspoon chicken bouillon
⅛ cup water
Garlic salt and fresh ground pepper to taste

In a small sauce pan using ⅛ cup water, simmer the frozen peas and the chicken bouillon on low heat, for three to five minutes—covered. Meanwhile, in a small nonstick frying pan, melt butter and sauté the minced onion lightly. Whisk in a little garlic salt and fresh pepper to taste. Pour over peas and gently stir. Then, while the peas are simmering, drizzle in the beaten egg. It gets scrambled and cooked. Serve hot.

Note: Paula made this side dish for our family often. Usually she served it as a go-along with pan fried pork chops or oven roasted chicken. Kick it up a notch by substituting the ⅛ cup of water with a "baby can" of Hunts Tomato Sauce. Rinse the can with a little water and add it to the recipe.

PEAS CREAMED 🍎
(Pois a La Sauce Crème)

Paula Grappo
Serves 4

1 small bag peas frozen
⅛ cup water
1 tablespoon butter

1 cup milk
Salt and pepper to taste

Simmer peas in a small sauce pan for three to five minutes, covered. Meanwhile, in a small nonstick frying pan, melt butter, sprinkle on the flour, and bubble lightly—being careful not to burn. Add milk and simmer on low until it thickens. Drain peas and add to the cream sauce. Salt and pepper the dish to taste. Serve hot.

Note: This recipe becomes an entire meal simply by adding one can of white tuna to the recipe. Heat and serve over toast! Makes a great main course any day of the week—or it's special for meatless days during Lent.

PINEAPPLE STUFFING 🎄

Kim Ross
Serves 12

½ cup butter
2 cups sugar
8 eggs
2 20 oz. cans crushed
  pineapple, drained

3 tablespoons lemon juice
10 slices white bread, day-old,
  cubed

In a mixer, cream butter and sugar until light and fluffy. Add the eggs, one at a time, beating well after each is added. Stir in pineapple and lemon juice by hand. Fold in bread cubes. Pour into a greased 13" x 9" baking dish. Bake, uncovered, at 325° for 35-40 minutes—or until a knife inserted near the center comes out clean.

Note: My cousin, Kim Ross, was great at hosting excellent barbecues and she also excelled at this pineapple stuffing. Everyone loved it any time of year she made it, but especially at Easter time with baked ham.

PLANTAINS 🌎
(Plátanos)

Bro. Joseph
Serves 4

4 plantains, firm and ripe   **Vegetable oil**

With a small, sharp knife, cut ends from each plantain. Slice through the peels and remove them. Cut the fruit into very thin slices, about 1/8 inch thick. In a large, deep skillet, heat oil (about 1/4 inch deep) and fry 12 to 15 plantain slices at a time for 2 to 3 minutes, or until golden, turning them over once. Use a slotted spoon or spatula to remove cooked slices and place them on paper towels to drain. Season the slices with salt. Plantain slices should be slightly crisp on the outside, but soft on the inside. The slices are best served immediately; however, they may be made one day in advance, cooled completely, and stored in an airtight container. Reheat plantain slices on a rack in a shallow baking pan at 350°F for 5 minutes, or until heated through.

Note: If we had to pick one ingredient that shouts "Cuban cooking," it would have to be the plantain. But for all their pride of ownership, Cubans can't claim plantains as their native plant. The fruit probably originated in India thousands of years ago and landed in the Caribbean via Spanish settlers.

POTATO PANCAKES ⊘
(Potato Latkes American-style)

Bro. Joseph
Serves 4

4 Yukon Gold or Russet potatoes (medium to large), peeled, boiled, and mashed with butter and milk (mashed potatoes)
2 eggs beaten

¼ cup flour and ¼ cup bread crumbs—blended together
Sea salt and pepper the flour and bread crumbs to taste
Canola or grape seed oil

If you are using yesterday's leftover mashed potatoes, they are probably cold and perfect for this recipe. If you are making the mashed potatoes now, make sure they are cold before moving on to the next step. Then, heat a large skillet with oil to medium-high heat. Form the mashed potatoes into "hamburger patties" and dip all sides in the egg mixture. Then, dip in the flour and bread crumbs. Place in the hot oil and crisp brown on both sides. Serve hot with apple sauce or a dollop of sour cream and sliced green onions. Goes well as a side dish for pork chops, seafood, and roasts.

Note: Latkes are potato pancakes that Ashkenazi Jews have prepared as part of the December Hanukkah festival since the mid-1800s, based on an older variant of the dish that goes back to at least the Middle Ages. Latkes need not necessarily be made from potatoes.

POTATOES MASHED WITH GARLIC ⊘
(Garlic Smashed New Red Potatoes with Skins)

Bro. Joseph
Serves 6 - 8

10 to 12 red new potatoes, washed and quartered
8 garlic cloves peeled

1 stick of butter
½ cup milk
Salt and pepper to taste

Boil new potatoes with garlic, salt, and enough water to cover. Once tender, drain water and mash with butter and milk, as well as salt and pepper to taste. Keeping the skins on adds texture and vitamins to this popular dish. Remember that overcooking or over-mashing creates a starchy and uninteresting end-product.

Note: Goes well with a meatloaf recipe, as well as Sunday pot roast, gravy, fried chicken and gravy, and braised meats. I learned this from Chef Andre, Coral Gables, Florida Country Club in the 1980s. It was popular in his 4-star, 4-diamond restaurant when he served his roasted and braised meat platters.

POTATOES PAN-FRIED 🌎
(Potatoes Lyonnaise)

Bro. Joseph
Serves 4 - 6

5 large potatoes, boiled "Al Dente" and refrigerated overnight (if possible)	2 tablespoons fresh parsley minced
1 large onion sliced	3 tablespoons olive oil
2 tablespoons fresh garlic minced	3 tablespoons butter
	Sea salt and fresh ground pepper to taste

After the potatoes have chilled (you can place them in an ice bath if time doesn't allow for overnight), pat dry and remove the skins. On a cutting board, using a sharp knife, cut the potatoes into ½ inch slices. Heat the oil and butter on medium-high heat, in a large nonstick frying pan. Sauté the sliced potatoes until lightly browned on both sides. Add the garlic, onion, and ground pepper and sauté until golden brown. Remove and place in a serving dish with fresh parsley and a sprinkle of sea salt and serve. Goes great with beef tenderloin steaks.

Note: This recipe of Lyonnaise potatoes is a French dish of sliced, pan-fried potatoes and thinly sliced onions, sautéed in butter with parsley. A simple combination of potatoes and onions can be absolutely extraordinary. Be sure to use real butter and fresh parsley!

POTATOES ROSEMARY ⊘
(Oven Roasted Potatoes with Rosemary)

Bro. Joseph
Serves 4 - 6

10 small red or white new potatoes, washed and cut in half or...	1 lemon
	Garlic salt
	Onion Salt
5 to 6 large potatoes, washed and cut into chunks	Fresh ground pepper
	Olive oil
1 palm dried rosemary	½ stick butter melted
1 handful fresh rosemary	¼ cup water

In a large mixing bowl, place washed potatoes or potato chunks (no need to dry them). Squeeze lemon over the potatoes (without seeds) and season well with garlic salt, onion salt, and ground pepper. Toss with melted butter and drizzles of olive oil. Place potatoes and water into a 9" x 13" glass baking dish and bake uncovered at 375 F for one hour or until golden brown and crispy. For the last 15 minutes, baste the potatoes with some of the drippings from the Rosemary Chicken recipe to add even more flavor.

Note: Serve with oven-roasted Rosemary Chicken recipe, garden salad, and vegetable side dish.

RAISIN SAUCE 🍴
(Holiday Ham Raisin Sauce)

Paula Grappo

½ cup brown sugar
3 tablespoons cornstarch
1½ cups water
1 cup raisins

1 tablespoon vinegar
1 tablespoon lemon juice
2 tablespoons butter
1 cup orange juice

In a medium-sized saucepan, combine all ingredients until blended. Bring to a low simmer and cook for two minutes or until thickened. Stir in butter until melted. Serve in a gravy boat (with ladle), as a side dish for holiday ham.

Note: Paula served Raisin Sauce as a side to Christmas and Easter hams. It was always a favorite tradition among family and guests.

RICE PERFECT ⊘
(Perfect Rice Every Time)

Bro. Joseph
Serves 4

1 cup Jasmine or Basmati rice
1.5 cups cold water

1 tablespoon butter
1 pinch sea salt

Using a colander, briefly rinse the rice under cold running water. Look for debris or stones and remove. Place the rice in a medium-sized sauce pan (with matching lid), along with water, butter, and salt. Cover and bring to a boil. In about five minutes, once it starts to simmer, turn off the heat. Leave pot on the stove—but do not open the lid. Set kitchen timer for 20 minutes. Transfer to a bowl and serve hot. Hint: double the recipe for leftovers.

Note: Leftover Jasmine or Basmati makes a wonderful cereal snack for big and little kids alike! Place a few spoonfuls of cold rice from the refrigerator in a cereal bowl. Next, pour milk and a few raisins over it. Top with a little sugar or honey and a few taps of cinnamon. Cover with a paper towel and warm in the microwave for 1-2 minutes. Serve hot for breakfast or a snack!

SCALLOPED POTATOES ★

Bro. Joseph
Serves 4 - 6

4 to 6 medium Russet or Gold Potatoes washed, peeled, and cut into round slices, pat dry with clean towel
1 medium onion peeled and chopped

Flour
Butter
Milk
Salt and ground pepper to taste

Preheat oven to 350 F. Pam spray 9" x 13" glass baking dish. Place a layer of potato slices that cover the bottom of the dish. Next, sprinkle some onion, a dusting of flour by the tablespoon, and lastly 4 to 5 dabs of butter squares. Now, sprinkle with sea salt and grinds of fresh ground pepper. Then, repeat a new layer beginning with spreading potato slices. Repeat more sprinkles of onion, flour, pads of butter, salt, and pepper. Repeat until all ingredients have been used up. Now, take your milk carton and freely pour milk in the center until you see it rise ½ way up the side. Stop. Cover with tinfoil and bake for 45 minutes. Then, remove cover and bake 15 minutes until bubbly and toasted brown on top. Remove from the oven, place on wire rack for 10 minutes and then cut into squares and serve.

Note: Excellent dish to serve with pan-fried fresh fish, baked lemon white fish, baked Easter ham, or a winter pot roast. Change it up by adding (for last 15 minutes—uncovered) fresh bread crumbs tossed in a little butter and browned under the broiler; and/or add minced crispy bacon sprinkled across the top with shreds of cheddar cheese until gooey and melted!

SPINACH CREAMED 🍎
(Spinach in Bechamel and Cream Cheese Sauce)

Bro. Joseph

1 large bag fresh spinach, washed and chopped
1 cup recipe of Bechamel Sauce (make half)

1 (small square or half package) Philadelphia Cream Cheese
Salt and pepper to taste

Sauté the spinach in a large skillet in ¼ cup of water over medium heat. Once wilted, drain water, add 1 cup Bechamel Sauce to the skillet—plus the Philadelphia Cream Cheese. Salt and pepper to taste. Serves well as a side dish for poultry and steak dinners. A bag of frozen spinach may be substituted for fresh spinach.

Note: Creamed spinach has a long history of German, French and Swiss European origins. In the United States it has found its way to garnish steaks at the popular and upscale Ruth's Chris Steak House.

VEGETABLE MEDLEY 🍎
(Steamed Vegetables with Cheddar Cheese Sauce)

- 1 large bag fresh vegetable medley (from produce department)
- 1 small bag cheddar cheese shredded
- 2 cups skim or regular milk
- 2 tablespoons butter
- 2 tablespoons all-purpose flour
- 1 teaspoon granulated chicken bouillon or garlic seasoning salt
- 4 to 8 grinds fresh pepper to taste

In a large sauce pan, add ¼ inch of water. Add vegetables, bring to a boil while covered well. Boil for three to four minutes until "Al Dente." (Just like the pasta!) Quickly drain in a sink colander. Set aside on a long serving platter. In a large skillet, melt butter on medium heat. Add flour and form a paste. Add milk, bouillon or garlic salt and ground pepper. Whisk constantly. Once the sauce begins to thicken, add cheddar cheese slowly until melted and blended. If the sauce is too thick, add a little more milk to lighten it up. Pour over vegetable platter and serve hot.

Main Dishes

MAIN DISHES

BEEF BRISKET OVEN ROASTED ⊘
(Beer Bottle Beef Brisket)

Bro. Joseph
Serves 6 - 8

1 12-oz. bottle beer
1 can cranberry sauce or whole cranberries
½ cup ketchup
2 tablespoons olive oil
4 to 5 lbs. flat-cut beef brisket, washed and patted dry
1 large onion sliced
Sea salt and fresh ground pepper

Preheat oven to 350 F. In a medium-size bowl, combine the beer, cranberry, and ketchup. Set aside. In a large sauce pot, add olive oil and beef brisket—seasoned with salt and pepper on all sides. Sear on medium-high heat. Rotate often, browning the exterior—about 10 minutes. Place beef brisket in a small roasting pan and cover with sliced onions and sauce. Transfer to oven and bake at 350 F until tender, or 2 to 3 hours. Before slicing, let meat cool for 15 minutes at room temperature. Serve with buttered or cream cheese noodles, vegetable side dish, and salad. Feel free to add extra cranberry sauce and onion according to taste.

Note: A friend in New York once commented, "I love this recipe so much, I made it twice in a week!"

BEEF ROAST IN RED WINE 🍷
(Rôti de Boeuf au Vin Rouge)

Bro. Joseph
Serves 5 - 8

5 lbs. chuck or top round roast, washed and patted dry
1 roll kitchen twine (optional)
1 cup carrots, peeled and chopped in chunks
1 cup celery, washed and chopped in chunks
1 cup white or yellow onion, peeled and cut in chunks
2 fresh tomatoes, washed and cut in chunks
1 bottle good red wine, Cabernet Sauvignon or Merlot
1 bouquet garni - one square of cheese cloth filled with bay leaf, pieces of chopped celery, parsley, thyme, cloves, garlic, and black pepper seeds—tied off into a "tea bag"
2 cups beef bouillon stock
3 tablespoons cornstarch
3 tablespoons Vermouth or white wine
Sea salt and pepper to taste

On the stove top, brown the roast in a large sauce pan with a little oil on all sides—at medium-high heat. Next, add a few more drops of cooking oil and sauté the vegetables for a few minutes until lightly cooked. Simmer the roast with the addition of the tomatoes, red wine, and beef stock, to cover the roast at least ½ to ⅔ high. Finally, add the bouquet garni and continue to simmer on low for 3 hours. Rotate the roast every hour. Before serving, remove the meat and set aside. Let the juice sit a minute and skim off excess grease and discard. Strain juices through a fine strainer—directly into a large clean frying pan. Now you can thicken the juices on medium heat with the blend of cornstarch and Vermouth. Thicken the sauce, thinly slice roast onto a serving tray, pour the sauce over it, and garnish with fresh parsley or thyme. Extra gravy may be served in a gravy boat with a side of boiled, baked, or mashed potatoes.

Note: The origins of this recipe are the provinces and wine country of southwest France. The recipe pairs well with a garden salad, San Francisco sourdough bread or European-style dark breads, and French or California red wines such as Cabernet Sauvignon, Merlot or red Zinfandel.

BEEF ROAST SWEET AND SAUCY 🍖
(Beef Roast, Brisket or Pork Tenderloin in a Crockpot)

Bro Joseph
Serves 6 - 8

2.5 lbs. Beef Roast or Pork Tenderloin
1 teaspoon salt
4 grinds of fresh pepper
1 12-oz. jar Heinz Chili Sauce
1 16-oz. can jellied cranberry sauce
2 tablespoons brown sugar

In a crockpot, combine chili sauce and cranberry sauce. Roll meat in salt and pepper. Place meat in the crockpot. Cover and cook on high for 1.5 hours or on low for 3 hours. Make the Day Before: Take 5 minutes the night before and mix all of the ingredients in the slow cooker and store in the fridge until ready to turn on. Garnish with fresh rosemary or fresh parsley. Serve with jasmine rice, baked or boiled potato, and additional sauce in a gravy boat on the side— along with a can of Ocean Spray chilled cranberry sauce.

Note: This recipe has been a Heinz favorite since the 1950s!

BEEF TENDERLOIN STEAKS 🍷
(Bifteck de Boeuf à la Sauce au Vin)

Bro. Joseph
Serves 4

4 tenderloin steaks (½" thick)
2 tablespoons olive oil
2 tablespoons butter
2 shallots or ½ white onion minced
½ cup good red wine
2 garlic cloves crushed
Fresh parsley minced
1 tablespoon butter additional

In a nonstick frying pan, sauté the steaks on medium-high heat in butter and olive oil. Sear 2 minutes on each side with a little pepper, onion, or garlic salt on each. Remove steaks and set aside. Quickly deglaze the sauce on medium-high heat by adding 1 tablespoon of butter, the minced shallots or onion, ½ cup red wine, and parsley. Once the sauce begins to evaporate, forming a saucy glaze, pour over the steaks and serve immediately.

Note: Deglazing is a cooking technique for removing and dissolving browned food particles from a pan to flavor sauces, soups, and gravies. The flavor is determined chiefly by the meat, the liquid used for deglazing, and any flavoring or finishing ingredients added, such as spices, herbs, or butter.

CHICKEN KOREAN 🌐
(Dalg hangug-eo)

- 8 chicken thighs or 8 pork chops thinly cut
- ¾ cup soy sauce or lite soy sauce
- 1 medium or large onion sliced
- ⅛ cup canola or sesame oil
- 3 tablespoons honey
- 5 garlic cloves minced
- 2 tablespoons ginger root fresh grated
- 1 teaspoon dried ginger
- 5 grounds fresh pepper

Preheat oven at 300 F. Arrange chicken or pork chops in a 9" x 13" glass baking dish. Peel ginger root and chop finely in an electric mini chopper. Then, peel garlic and chop finely in the mini chopper. Combine all other ingredients in a bowl and lightly whisk to form a sauce. Drizzle this sauce all over the meat, carefully coating each piece. Bake uncovered for 3 hours. Sprinkle with sesame seeds and broil for 10 to 15 minutes. If gravy is too watery, pour into a frying pan on medium heat. Make ¼ cup water with 3 tablespoons corn starch. Add a tablespoon at a time for desired thickness and pour back over the meat dish. Serve with Jasmine or Basmati white or brown rice.

Note: A Korean woman from a Baptist church in Southwest, United States introduced this dish to me at a church potluck special for our college choir which was on tour at the time. The recipe has been a hit among family and friends for more than 40 years!

CHICKEN ROSEMARY ✠
(Roasted Chicken Rosemary with Lemon)

Bro. Joseph
Serves 4 -6

1 whole chicken, washed in/out and patted dry	Fresh ground pepper
1 palm full dried rosemary	½ stick of butter
1 handful fresh rosemary	¼ cup water
1 whole lemon	1 whole onion
Garlic salt	8 garlic cloves
	Olive oil

Place whole chicken in a roasting pan after using non-stick cooking spray. Generously season inside and out with garlic salt, fresh ground pepper, and dried and fresh rosemary. Pour ¼ cup of water in the bottom of the roasting pan. Squeeze one half of the lemon inside and one half of the lemon all over the outside. Stuff the interior with one half of the leftover lemon, ½ the onion, and ½ the garlic. Dot the outside with pads of butter tucking around wings and legs. Do the same with the rest of the garlic and slices of onion. Sprinkle lightly with olive oil. Place in preheated oven at 375 F—uncovered for one hour and 20 minutes, until golden brown. Baste the chicken after 45 minutes, 60 minutes, and about every 5 minutes thereafter until done. Serve with roasted rosemary potatoes, garden salad, and vegetable.

Note: The safe internal temperature for cooked chicken is 165 F (75° Celsius). A meat or instant-read thermometer is your best bet for determining the temperature of your chicken.

CHIMICHURRI SAUCE ⟩
(Gaucho-Style Argentinian Chimichurri Sauce)

Luis Rimoli
Serves 6

½ cup olive oil
¼ cup malt or balsamic vinegar
¼ cup parsley finely chopped
3 to 4 garlic cloves finely chopped
1 teaspoon cayenne pepper
¼ cup fresh basil, cilantro, or oregano—finely chopped
1 tablespoon sea salt
3 to 4 grinds pepper (or more to taste)
⅛ cup water

Mix all ingredients together in a bowl. Allow to sit for 24 hours at room temperature. In Argentina, Chimichurri is usually prepared a day ahead of time. Use it to baste meats (chicken or steaks) while grilling, baking, broiling, or barbecuing. You can also use it as an overnight meat marinade. Serve it in a small dish for guests to garnish meats, just as they would use A-1 or bottled hot sauce.

Note: Chimichurri is a loose, oil-based dressing or salsa, used to accompany barbecued, oven-roasted, or braised meats. It's also used as a marinade for poultry, fish, pork, and beef. Chimichurri is a popular tradition from the gauchos (cowboys) of Uruguay and Argentina—and is considered the best accompaniment to any barbecued or grilled meats.

FISH PAN-SEARED ♥
(Poisson Cuit à la Sauce Herbe Fraîche)

Bro. Joseph
Serves 4

- 1 large boneless cod, halibut, or haddock fillet cut into four 6 oz. pieces
- 2 tablespoons butter
- 2 tablespoons canola or olive oil
- 1 small onion finely chopped
- 2 garlic cloves minced
- ⅛ cup white wine
- 1 teaspoon fresh lemon juice
- ½ cup heavy cream
- Salt and fresh pepper to taste
- 3 small tomatoes chopped finely
- 1 teaspoon each of fresh herbs, such as basil, thyme, sage, chives, parsley, etc.
- ¼ cup capers (optional)

Optional: marinade the fish overnight in the juice of one whole lemon, olive oil, fresh ground black pepper, fresh herbs, and a little minced garlic and onion. Next day: in a a large skillet, melt butter and olive oil on medium-high heat and sear the fish 2 minutes on each side. Quickly place in a 9" x 13" glass baking dish and set aside in the oven at 250 F. Then, add a little extra butter to the pan, lower the heat to medium and sauté the onion and garlic until soft—but not brown. Add the wine, stir, and let it cook down briefly. Then stir in the cream. Raise the heat so the liquid thickens a bit, then stir in the tomatoes. Cook over high heat another minute or so, just until the tomatoes soften. Then add the herbs. Season the sauce to taste with salt and pepper or a teaspoon of chicken bouillon. Add the lemon juice. Spoon over fish and serve with garnish of fresh herbs over the top of the platter. Hint: double the sauce recipe and have extra to pour over a side of pasta. Serve a side of asparagus "Al Dente" with drizzles of melted butter and squeezes of fresh lemon.

Note: Double the recipe and it works well for large family gatherings (cut the pieces of fish smaller at 3 oz each). The fish stays hot for a long time in the glass baking dish, when served buffet-style with other dishes.

IRISH OATMEAL BOWL ♥
(Quaker Oats for Breakfast, Lunch or Dinner)

Bro. Joseph
Serves 4

4 servings Quaker Oats recipe (according to box)	1 cup walnuts chopped
1 large apple, cored and chopped	4 teaspoons cinnamon
	4 tablespoons butter or margarine
1 cup dark or golden raisins (dried cranberries may be substituted)	1 cup buttermilk
	1 cup brown sugar or Splenda brown sugar

Divide hot oatmeal evenly into 4 serving bowls. Dot each with 1 tablespoon of butter or margarine. Next, sprinkle each bowl with 1 teaspoon of cinnamon, ¼ cup walnuts, ¼ cup raisins, ¼ cup of apple chunks and ¼ cup of brown sugar. Then, pour ¼ cup buttermilk in the center of each bowl. Serve immediately with hot coffee, tea, hot chocolate, cold milk, or juice.

Note: Think again—oatmeal is not just for breakfast! Try serving this hearty meal in a bowl for lunch, dinner, or as a powerful start to a hard-working morning. Heart healthy oatmeal can lower cholesterol if eaten frequently as part of a healthy diet.

ITALIAN FRIED CHICKEN ✠
(With Mashed Potatoes and Gravy)

James Grappo Sr.
Serves 6 - 8

2 packs (2 lbs. each) skinless chicken thighs and the other skinless drumsticks
¼ cup Crisco
⅛ cup Canola oil
Onion powder
Garlic powder
Dried oregano
Dried basil
Sea salt and pepper to taste

10 cloves of garlic, peeled and cut lengthwise in half
Gravy
1 cup chicken bouillon broth made with two cubes
1 cup milk
2 rounded tablespoons flour
Fresh ground pepper
2 tablespoons butter

In a large nonstick frying pan, melt Crisco and oil together. In a large mixing bowl, pat dry chicken pieces. Next, season them heavily with sliced garlic, onion powder, garlic powder, oregano, basil, salt, and pepper. Mix by hand—coating all sides with the seasonings. Arrange in frying pan on medium-high heat. Fry each side until crispy brown. Remove and set aside in a glass serving platter in the oven at 200 F. Now reduce heat to medium-low, adding the 2 tablespoons of butter and two tablespoons of flour until melted together. Next, add 1 cup double-strength chicken bouillon and 1 cup milk. Add ground pepper. Stir until thickens and then transfer to a gravy boat with ladle and serve hot with fried chicken and mashed potatoes. A side of spaghetti or buttered corn also goes well with this dinner.

ITALIAN PIZZA 🌐
(Homemade Deep Dish Pizza)

Bro. Joseph
Serves 4 - 6

1 Bread Basic recipe	Olive oil
1 onion minced	Sea salt and pepper
1 bell pepper sliced julienne	Dried oregano and basil
1 large tomato chopped	Crisco
½ cup fresh mushrooms sliced	6 slices of bacon, cut into one
1 small bag mozzarella cheese shredded	inch pieces with scissors and fried and until crispy

Let rise until double one Basic Bread recipe. Preheat oven to 425 F. Heavily grease two 9-inch round cake pans—sides and bottom—with Crisco. Cut dough in half and spread across the bottom of each pan with hands, palms, and fingers. Next, season top of dough lightly with salt and pepper. Sprinkle half of the vegetables and bacon bits on each. Season again with salt, pepper, oregano, and basil. Lightly drizzle bacon drippings over the top of each pizza. Bake about 20 minutes or until bottom is crispy brown when lifted with a spatula. Do not burn!

Note: In Italy pizzas are made many different ways. Try the above recipe with sea salt, drizzles of olive oil, and minced fresh and/or dried rosemary—creating a flatbread focaccia. Another Italian favorite is chopped fried zucchini scrambled with eggs and spread over a pizza dough with Parmesan and/or Mozzarella cheese. All pizzas can be the main dish or side to soup or salad.

MEATLOAF AMERICAN STYLE 🌎
(Pâté Américan)

Bro. Joseph
Serves 4

2 lbs ground turkey, chicken, beef, or combination
1 egg
¼ cup bread crumbs or oatmeal
1 teaspoon garlic salt or sea salt
8 grinds fresh pepper
1 teaspoon thyme, fresh minced or ground

Gravy
1 can Campbell's Cream of Mushroom Soup
1 small can mushrooms
½ cup milk
½ pack Lipton Onion Soup Mix

Preheat oven to 350 F. In a large mixing bowl, combine all the ingredients for the pâté. Form mixture into a meatloaf and place in a small roasting pan with non-stick cooking spray. Set aside. In a large mixing bowl combine the ingredients for the gravy and whisk together. Pour over the meatloaf, cover, and bake for 60 to 80 minutes. Remove cover and baste with spoon the last 10 minutes. Serve with rice or mashed potatoes. Next day, try serving it cold as a lunchtime sandwich on buttered bread—topped with a thin spread of ketchup.

Note: Who knew meatloaf wasn't just the invention of post-war thrifty moms? It turns out the idea of mixing meat with fillers traces back to about the year 400 AD, when the Roman cookbook Apicius presented a recipe of ground meat mixed with bread, wine, and formed into patties. By the 1800s, the French refined it into pâté and Americans made meatloaf.

PASTA AND MEATBALLS ⓧ
(Pasta e Polpette)

Sarah Sylvester
Serves 6

- 1 recipe of bolognese sauce (set ground meat aside in a bowl)
- ¼ onion finely chopped
- 1 egg
- ¾ cup breadcrumbs and/or Saltine cracker crumbs
- ½ teaspoon each: garlic powder, onion powder, oregano, and pepper
- 1.5 teaspoon salt
- ¼ cup Italian Parmesan cheese

Make your recipe of bolognese sauce. Omit the meat and divert it to a bowl with all the above ingredients. Mix by hand. Add more bread crumbs if too wet. Now, form small to medium-sized meatballs, lay them in a baking dish with non-stick cooking spray and bake at 350 F for 20 minutes. Spoon into the sauce and simmer on very low for one to three hours. Stir often. Serve with your favorite "Al Dente" spaghetti, linguine, angel hair pasta, shells, rigatoni, etc. Or, make the homemade pasta recipe in this book.

Note: Aunt Sarah loved to make grandma's sauce and meatball recipe. Sundays was the same thing, spaghetti, and in broken Italian she would say, "ball-a-meat!" We did not mind because it was so good and made with so much love that it always was like eating it for the first time. She served it with a simple lettuce and a little tomato, tossed with olive oil, vinegar and salt.

PASTA AND SPINACH GREENS 🍎
(Pasta e Spinaci Verdi)

Bro. Joseph

- 1 large bag triple washed spinach or swiss chard greens chopped
- 2 28-oz. cans tomato sauce, purée or crushed
- 6 garlic cloves minced
- 1 small onion minced
- 1 tablespoon salt
- 1 tablespoon sugar
- 1 teaspoon dried oregano
- 1 teaspoon dried basil
- 1 teaspoon pepper
- ¼ cup olive oil

In a large sauce pot, sauté in olive oil the greens, onion, and garlic until wilted (frozen spinach, peas, or other greens may be substituted). Quickly add cans of tomatoes. Rinse each can half full of water and add to the pot. Add seasonings and simmer 1 hour or less.

Note: Serve on meatless days during Lent or anytime of year as a vegetarian dish. Prepare your favorite pasta, spaghetti, or gnocchi according to package directions, "Al Dente." Drain and mix in family serving bowl with 1 to 2 cups of sauce. Serve remaining sauce on the side with Italian Parmesan cheese and red pepper flakes.

PASTA BOLOGNESE SAUCE ♥
(Ground Meat Sauce)

Bro. Joseph

2 lbs. ground turkey, chicken, or beef	1 tablespoon dried oregano
1 small onion chopped finely	1 teaspoon dried basil
6 garlic cloves chopped finely	1 teaspoon black pepper
2 28-oz. cans tomato purée, sauce or crushed	1 tablespoon sugar
	1 tablespoon garlic salt
	¼ cup olive oil

In a large skillet, fry the ground meat in a little vegetable oil. Sprinkle ground meat with garlic salt. Once cooked, set aside. Next, in a large spaghetti pot, fry chopped onion and garlic in the olive oil until light brown. Quickly add the 2 cans of tomatoes. Rinse each can half full with water and pour into the pot. Add all ingredients and simmer 1 to 3 hours on low heat. Stir often.

Note: Serve with your choice of spaghetti, linguine, gnocchi, shells, bow ties, angel hair, etc. Be sure to cook the pasta "Al Dente" according to package directions. Drain pasta, place in family serving bowl, add 1 or 2 cups of sauce, stir, and serve a bowl of sauce on the side with a ladle. Also, offer Italian Parmesan cheese and dried crushed red pepper on the side.

PASTA COTTAGE CHEESE 🍎
(Pasta e Ricotta)

Bro. Joseph

1 small tub cottage cheese or ricotta cheese	½ stick butter

Make your favorite pasta, spaghetti, or gnocchi "Al Dente" according to package instructions. Drain and set aside in a colander. Next, melt butter in the bottom of the pot on low heat and add the pasta and cottage cheese or ricotta. Mix and warm thoroughly and pour into family serving bowl. Garnish with any of the following on the side: minced fresh chives or green onions, poppy seeds, fresh basil or parsley. Serve with Italian Parmesan cheese and dried red pepper flakes.

Note: Add a salad to this dish and a homemade, nutritious family dinner will be prepared and served in under 15 minutes! Experiment with flavors and variations by adding a little garlic salt, minced garlic, onion, or a teaspoon of oregano to the butter and cottage cheese.

PASTA OR BROCCOLI WITH GARLIC AND OLIVE OIL
(Pasta or Broccoli Aglio e Olio)

Bro. Joseph
Serves 4 - 6

2 heads of broccoli or one pound of pasta cooked "Al Dente"	8 garlic cloves, peeled and minced in an electric mini chopper
⅓ cup olive oil	Sea salt and pepper to taste

If you are making just "Broccoli with Garlic and Olive Oil," separate the broccoli and boil in one inch of water covered for 5 minutes. Drain and set aside. In a large nonstick frying pan, fry the oil and garlic until light brown. Now throw in the broccoli and toss with sea salt and fresh ground pepper. Serve hot. Note: You can also combine the broccoli dish and pasta dish (like shells or bow ties) and then toss it together in garlic and olive oil sauce. If needed, you can always drizzle more olive oil or squeeze a little fresh lemon if the dish becomes too dry.

Note: If you are making "Pasta Aglio e Olio," cook the spaghetti like angel hair, linguine, or gnocchi until "Al Dente." Drain and set aside. In a large nonstick pan, fry oil and garlic until light brown. Now toss in the spaghetti, sea salt, and pepper. Serve with Parmesan. Excellent for meatless days during Lent.

PASTA TUNA SAUCE ♥
(PASTA SALSA TONNO)

Jo Celio

2 28-oz. cans tomato purée, sauce or crushed	1 tablespoon sugar
2 large cans white tuna, packed in water or oil	1 tablespoon salt
	1 teaspoon black pepper
	1 tablespoon dried oregano
6 garlic cloves finely chopped	1 teaspoon dried basil
1 small onion finely chopped	¼ cup olive oil

In a large sauce pot, sauté the garlic and onion in olive oil until golden brown. Quickly add the two cans of tomatoes, plus rinse each can half full with water and add to the pot. Add the tuna fish and seasonings. Simmer on low for 1 to 2 hours.

Note: For the season of Lent, or other meatless days, serve with your favorite spaghetti, pasta or gnocchi. Cook the pasta "Al Dente" according to instructions. Drain and mix in a family serving bowl with 1 or 2 cups of sauce. Serve additional sauce on the side, along with Italian Parmesan cheese and dried red pepper. (Clams Marinara - substitute tuna with 3 cans minced clams.)

POACHED EGGS IN CHEESE SAUCE SPINACH GARNISH ✠
(Oeufs au Sauce Fromage)

Bro. Joseph
Serves 4

4 large or extra large fresh eggs
1 small sauce pan of boiling water with tablespoon of vinegar
4 English muffins or bread slices toasted
1 cup ham minced or bacon bits (optional)

1 cup milk
1 tablespoon flour
6 oz. (or more) cheddar cheese shredded
1 tablespoon butter
Sea salt and fresh ground pepper to taste

Place the water/vinegar mixture in a small nonstick sauce pan. Bring to a light boil. First make your sauce also in a nonstick frying pan by melting butter and flour to form a paste. Add milk and bring to a low simmer. With a helper, have one person stir while another adds the shredded cheese—until it melts into the sauce. Remove from the burner and set aside. Carefully crack 4 eggs into the simmering water (do not stir or touch). Boil at a medium simmer for 3 to 4 minutes. Remove quickly with a slotted spoon and place on paper towels. Now, place toasted and buttered English muffins (or bread) on each person's plate. Top with a poached egg, cheese sauce, and hot bacon and/or ham bits. Serve with parsley or other fresh herb garnish. You can also garnish this dish and make it meatless by using fresh spinach leaves that are washed and blanched 5 seconds in simmering hot water.

Note: This dish is great for weekend mornings, Sunday brunch, or weeknights as a main course. Serves well with home ground coffee, glass of fresh-squeezed orange juice, and homemade fruit salad drizzled with hand-whisked lemon and honey dressing. Got extra hungry hombres in the house? Make a skillet of potato, pepper, and onion home fries.

SHREDDED TURKEY OR CHICKEN BAKE ⊙
(Thanksgiving Leftovers Casserole All Year Around)

Bro. Joseph
Serves 4 - 6

3 cups chicken or turkey shredded
1 10-oz. can cream of mushroom soup
¼ cup sour cream
½ cup milk
1 small can mushrooms drained
1 6-oz. box Stove Top Stuffing

First, make Stove Top Stuffing according to box instructions. Add a little minced onion, celery, rosemary, sage, and thyme (optional), and set aside. In a mixing bowl, combine shredded chicken or turkey along with cream of mushroom soup, mushrooms, milk, and sour cream. Gently stir and pour into a 9" x 13" glass baking dish, spray bottom with non-stick cooking spray. Sprinkle stuffing on top. Bake uncovered at 375 F for 25 to 30 minutes—until bubbly at the bottom. Serve with chilled cranberry sauce and garden salad on the side.

Note: One of the "Church Ladies" made this dish in Scottsdale, AZ when our college choir was on tour in 1975. Lucky to have received the recipe from her and to now share it with all of you!

SPAGHETTI PASTA HOMEMADE 🌎
(Pasta Fresca)

Jim Grappo Sr.
Serves 4

10 eggs
½ cup oil
½ cup water
1 teaspoon salt

4 to 5 large cookie trays
10 to 12 cups all-purpose flour
and/or Italian semolina flour

Whip eggs for 10 minutes in the electric mixer, beginning on low speed and gradually moving to high. Next, lower speed and slowly add remaining ingredients. Whip on high for another minute. Remove whisk and add the dough hook. Gradually add 10 to 12 cups of flour. Be sure to form a very hard ball. No tackiness left whatsoever. Cover with a clean towel and let dough rest 10 minutes. Using a rolling pin, level dough into 1-inch high, oblong shape. Cut into 1 inch strips. Use a lot of flour to run strips through spaghetti machine flat rollers, set thickness at #2. Next, run it through noodle cutting rollers set at #4. Lay noodles long ways in floured cookie sheets and use a lot of extra flour to keep them separated so they don't glue back together. Cook immediately for 2 to 3 minutes in salted boiling water or store at room temperature in cookie trays—allowing them to become dry and hard. They can be used the next day. No time to make sauce? Try serving them with butter and Parmesan cheese. Add sea salt and fresh ground pepper to taste on the side.

Note: Homemade pasta was our tradition to have Christmas Eve and served, "Aglio E Olio". Lightly sauté 10 cloves of fresh sliced garlic (don't burn) in ¼ to ½ cup of olive oil. Pour over pasta, toss, and serve.

SPANISH TORTILLA 🌎
(Tortilla de España)

Bro. Joseph
Serves 4 - 6

1 ¼ lbs. potatoes (3 to 4 medium)
1 medium onion sliced
1 cup olive oil
Sea salt and pepper to taste

1 small zucchini chopped
6 jumbo eggs lightly scrambled
1 small bell pepper green or red chopped

Peel and thinly slice potatoes and onions. Meanwhile, heat oil in an 8- or 10-inch nonstick skillet over medium heat. After 3 or 4 minutes, drop in a potato slice. When tiny bubbles appear around its edges, add potatoes, onions, a good pinch of salt, and a liberal sprinkling of pepper. Gently turn mixture in oil with a wooden spoon, and adjust heat so oil bubbles cook. Turn potatoes gently every few minutes, until they are tender when pierced with a small knife. Adjust the heat so they do not turn dark brown. If potatoes begin to break, they are overdone; stop cooking immediately. As potatoes cook, beat eggs with some salt and pepper in a large bowl. Drain potatoes in a colander, reserving oil. Wipe out skillet, and heat over a medium flame for a minute. Add 4 tablespoons oil. Gently mix warm potatoes, bell pepper, onion and zucchini. Once tender, then add eggs to skillet. As soon as edges firm up, after a minute or so, reduce heat to medium-low. Cook 5 minutes. Insert a rubber spatula all around edges of tortilla to make sure it will slide from pan. The top will still be runny. Carefully slide onto a plate. Cover with another plate, and—holding plates tightly—invert them. Add another tablespoon of oil to skillet, and use the spatula to coax tortilla back in. Cook 5 minutes, then slide from skillet onto a clean plate. Serve warm (not hot), or at room temperature. Do not refrigerate.

Note: I first learned this recipe with Greg Salazar, a violinist living among the gypsies in the 1970s. It was in a deserted village in the north of Spain, around Burgos and Saragoza. The recipe is popular in the Pyrenees, served between 10 pm and midnight, with a fresh French baguette and small glasses of red table wine and lots of lively music.

STUFFED CABBAGE 🌎
(Polish Stuffed Cabbages)

Paula Grappo
Serves 4 - 6

2 lbs. ground turkey, beef, or lamb
1 small onion minced
2 cups rice cooked drained and cooled

1 large head of cabbage
1 can tomatoes crushed
2 garlic cloves crushed
Salt, pepper, seasonings to taste

Sauté the ground meat in a large frying pan. Season with onion salt, garlic salt, paprika, chili powder, and black pepper to taste. Pour into a large bowl adding the cooked rice, minced onion, and garlic. Set aside. Boil cabbage in a large sauce pan with plenty of water. As the leaves turn a bright green, use a fork and knife to cut leaves from the core and place in a dish drainer to cool. Once you have removed all leaves, pour ½ of the crushed tomatoes in the bottom of a 9" x 13" glass baking dish. Line the bottom with leaves that are meat stuffed, rolled, and tucked in ends (with your fingers) cabbage rolls. Pour the remaining crushed tomatoes over the top and dot with butter pads or sprinkle with olive oil. Bake, covered with tinfoil, at 350 F for one hour. Serve with salad, mashed potatoes, and fresh bread. For an authentic German twist, you can also top this recipe with one small can of well-drained sauerkraut and then put crushed tomatoes and pads of butter on top. Not sure how to tightly roll cabbage rolls? Check YouTube!

Note: Paula learned this recipe from a Polish woman at church and made it often. Also, you can substitute cabbage for cored bell peppers, making "Stuffed Peppers!" Fill with the same meat and rice stuffing as above, crushed tomatoes on top and bottom, cover, and bake at 350 F for one hour or until tender.

TARTAR SAUCE ☯
(Homemade Seafood Tartar Sauce)

Bro. Joseph

1 cup mayonnaise or Miracle Whip
¼ cup (or more) dill or sweet relish

1 teaspoon onion minced (optional)

In a small mixing bowl, combine ingredients by hand. Spoon into a small dip bowl. Serve on the side with your favorite baked, fried seafood, or fish. Add color to the sauce by garnishing the top with some minced fresh parsley, basil, chives, or green onions.

Note: Whether it's a pack of Gorton's freezer case seafood or fish sticks that you may be serving, or your own fresh-baked lemon and butter white fish, this tartar sauce is faster, cheaper, and easier than those you can buy in the store.

WHITE SAUCE
(Bechamel Sauce)

Bro. Joseph

2 cups milk
2 tablespoons butter
2 tablespoons all-purpose flour

2 to 4 grinds of pepper
1 teaspoon sea salt

In a large skillet, melt butter on medium heat. Add flour and form a paste. Add milk, salt, and ground pepper. Whisk constantly. Once the sauce begins to thicken, use as needed for creamed peas, creamed spinach, string beans, or other recipes that call for Bechamel sauce. It is optional to add cheddar cheese, Velveeta cheese (pour over elbow noodles and bake for "Mac 'N Cheese"), or Italian Parmesan cheese and shredded Mozzarella, (pour over pasta for ("Spaghetti Alfredo").

Breads & Rolls

BREADS & ROLLS

APPLE FRITTERS ★
(All American Apple Fritters)

Paula Grappo
Serves 6 - 8

1 cup flour
1 teaspoon baking powder
1 teaspoon salt
4 tablespoons sugar
2 eggs separated

½ cup milk
1 teaspoon vegetable oil
6 medium apples, peeled, carefully cored and cut into ¼ inch rings

Combine and stir flour, baking powder, salt, and sugar. Beat the egg yolks and milk and blend with the flour. Beat egg whites until stiff. Lightly fold into the mixture. Heat a frying pan on medium-high heat with approximately ¼ cup vegetable oil, keeping the oil shallow. Dip apple rings in batter and fry on each side, turning with a fork until brown. Drain on paper towels and sprinkle with powdered sugar. Makes about 24 fritters. You can also experiment with this recipe by chopping the apples into small chunks, blending them into the batter, and dropping (by tablespoon) into hot oil in a small sauce pan until brown. Use a slotted spoon to remove. Place on paper towels and sprinkle with powdered sugar.

Note: Paula made these in the fall after we made picking apples at the orchards—an annual September and October family tradition. The many bushels of apples keep well in a cold basement or attic for most of the winter, but be careful to remove bad apples from time to time.

BANANA BREAD
(Quick Bread)

Dolores Grappo
Serves 4

½ cup Canola oil
1 cup sugar
2 cups flour
2 eggs
¾ teaspoon baking soda
½ teaspoon baking powder

¼ cup milk
½ cup walnuts chopped
¼ teaspoon salt
2 bananas mashed
1 teaspoon vanilla

In an electric mixer, whisk oil, sugar, eggs, vanilla, and beat well. Add mashed bananas and milk. By hand or with the paddle attachment, stir in flour, baking powder, salt, and baking soda. Fold in walnuts on low speed. Bake in Pam spray greased loaf pan at 350 F for about 45 minutes to 1 hour. Let cool in pan on cooling rack. Remove, place on a serving dish, and glaze with drizzles of powdered sugar and water.

Note: Banana bread is versatile, allowing for personal creativity. Try folding ½ cup of chocolate or butterscotch chips into the batter. Or, fold in ½ cup of raisins with just the walnuts. For a fall seasonal twist, try substituting one banana for ½ cup pumpkin purée for "Banana Pumpkin Bread."

BREAD BASIC RECIPE ⊘
(Italian Bread and Rolls)

Bro. Joseph
Makes two medium loafs of bread or 6 rolls.

- 1 ¼ cups lukewarm water
- 1 teaspoon salt
- 1 tablespoon sugar
- 1 package fresh Fleischman's Active Dry or Rapid Rise Yeast
- 1 heaping tablespoon vital wheat gluten or whole wheat flour
- 2 tablespoons butter softened
- 2 heaping tablespoons powdered milk or powdered buttermilk
- 3 cups all-purpose Gold Medal Flour or King Arthur Bread Flour + extra tablespoons of flour as needed to form a ball

Combine all ingredients in a Kitchen Aid Mixer using the dough hook or a bread machine using the dough cycle. Or, mix all ingredients by hand in a mixing bowl to form a medium-soft ball, turn onto a floured surface and knead 5 minutes. Or use a Kitchen Aid Mixer with dough hook until forming a soft ball and knead by machine for 5 minutes. Let rise, covered, in a clean bowl for one hour. Take out and knead on a counter top surface for one minute. Preheat oven to 350 F. Form bread loaves and place in two well-greased (use Crisco or Pam) bread loaf pans. Or, divide dough into 6 equal pieces and place each in a well-greased muffin pan. Cover with a clean dish towel and let rise about 30 minutes in a warm, draft-free area. Optional is to brush tops with a beaten egg. Bake for 20 to 30 minutes, or until golden brown and the top taps hollow. Remove from oven, butter tops (if they do not have an egg wash) and let cool at least 10 minutes before serving. Serve with soup, salads, and meats—along with your favorite butter, margarine, jams, and honey.

Note: You will also use this basic bread recipe frequently in the St. Joseph's Inn Cookbook to make Cinnamon Bread, Cinnamon Rolls, Raisin Bread, Raisin Rolls, Flatbread Italian Focaccia, Zeppole - Italian Pastry, Pizza, and more. Be sure to use yeast that has not expired!

BREAD FLAT 🌎
(Focaccia)

Bro. Joseph

1 Bread Basic Recipe
½ cup olive oil
⅓ cup fresh rosemary chopped
  or 4 tablespoons dried
  rosemary

Sea Salt or Coarse Kosher Salt

Preheat oven to 400 F. Prepare two 9-inch round cake pans by greasing heavily with Crisco. Divide dough into two sections and spread evenly by hand across the cake pans. Next use your finger tips to press shallow "pot holes" all over the dough. Then, sprinkle with equal parts of rosemary and olive oil. Use rock salt to taste. Bake 10 to 15 minutes until crispy brown.

Note: Serve rosemary-style focaccia with a glass of beer or wine—along with cheese, olives, and other appetizers or as a side to main dishes like soups, salads, and pastas. Cold leftover focaccia warms well in a 400 F oven for just 5 minutes. Also, rosemary may be substituted for chopped fresh basil, garlic, onion, sliced olives, anchovies, or Parmesan cheese.

BREAD FOR ST. PATRICK'S DAY ☘
(Irish Soda Bread)

Mille Failte
Serves 4

2 cups flour
1 teaspoon each - baking
  powder and baking soda
4 tablespoons sugar
3 tablespoons butter softened

1 cup buttermilk
1 egg beaten
1 cup raisins, plumped in warm
  water 10 minutes and drained
  well

Preheat oven to 375 F. Mix dry ingredients and combine with the wet ingredients—along with the raisins. Turn out onto a floured board. Knead, adding a little flour if necessary, until smooth and not sticky. Shape into a round loaf and cut a cross in the top. Place on a greased cookie sheet. Bake until brown on top and loaf taps hollow, about 45 minutes. Brush the top with butter once taken out of the oven.

Note: Paula received this recipe in 1970 from Mille Failte at the St. Patrick's Day Church Dinner and Dance.

BREAD FOR TOASTING
(English Muffin Bread)

Bro. Joseph
Serves 6 - 8

5 cups flour	¼ teaspoon baking soda
2 packages Fleischman's Rapid Rise Yeast	2 cups warm milk (100°)
	½ cup warm water (100°)
1 tablespoon sugar	Cornmeal
2 teaspoons salt	

Preheat oven to 350. In a large bowl, combine 2 cups flour, yeast, sugar, salt, and baking soda. Add warm milk and water; beat with a paddle on low-speed in a Kitchen Aid electric mixer for 30 seconds, scraping bowl occasionally. Beat on high for 3 minutes. Stir in remaining flour with the paddle attachment (batter will be stiff). Do not knead. Grease well bottom and sides of two 8-in. x 4-in. loaf pans. Sprinkle pans with cornmeal. Pour half the batter in each and bake 20 - 30 minutes or until golden on top and toothpick comes out clean. Remove from the oven. Place on wire rack to cool. Take a knife to loosen the sides, remove and let cool longer before slicing and toasting

Note: The English muffin, first called a "toaster crumpet," was invented in 1894 by a British immigrant to New York, Samuel Bath Thomas. English muffins were first exported to England by Thomas's in the 1990s. On that note, enjoy this bread with all its buttery nooks and crannies for a special holiday breakfast or, for that matter, any time of the year with family and friends.

BREAD WITH CINNAMON AND RAISINS [a]
(Cinnamon and Raisin Bread)

Bro. Joseph
Makes 2 medium loafs or 6 rolls

1 bread basic recipe	1 bottle cinnamon
½ stick butter softened	½ cup raisins or golden raisins
½ cup brown sugar or ¼ cup Splenda Brown Sugar Blend	(optional)

After the first rise, with a rolling pin on a lightly floured surface, form a rectangle ½-inch thick. Spread soft butter with hands or butter knife across the rectangle. Next, do the same with the brown sugar and sprinkle the top generously with cinnamon. Optional is to sprinkle the dough with ½ cup of raisins that have been soaked in warm water for 20 minutes and drained. Now roll the rectangle horizontal in front of you, careful to tuck the roll under as you form a long log. Cut in half and form 2 bread loaves and place in two well-greased (use Crisco or Pam) bread-loaf-pans. Or, with a sharp knife, cut the log into 6 equal pieces and place each in a well-greased muffin pan. Cover with a clean dish towel and let rise about 30 minutes in a warm, draft-free area. Optional is to brush tops with a beaten egg. Bake at 350 F for 20 to 30 minutes or until golden brown and the top taps hollow. Remove from oven. Butter tops if they do not have an egg wash and let cool 10 minutes or more before serving. Serve for breakfast, brunch, or dessert—along with your favorite butter, margarine, jams, and honey.

Note: Cinnamon bread and cinnamon raisin bread have been Christmastime favorites for hundreds of years in Europe and the United States. When the weather turns cold, it is the ideal recipe to bring comfort and warmth to family and friends who are escaping the chill of fall or the winter's snow. Serve with freshly-made hot coffee or your favorite tea.

BRUSCHETTA 🌎
(Italian Bread with Tomato and Basil)

Bro. Joseph
Appetizer Serves 6 - 10
Makes 24 Small Slices

7 ripe plum tomatoes chopped
3 teaspoons garlic minced (use an electric mini chopper)
Extra virgin olive oil
A small bunch of fresh basil chopped

1 baguette French bread or Italian bread, sliced (day-old is even better)
Sea salt and fresh ground pepper to taste

Preheat oven to 450 F. To thinly slice basil leaves, stack the leaves on top of each other and roll up like a cigar. Then, with kitchen scissors make thin slices from one end of the basil cigar to the other. Next, in a medium bowl combine the chopped tomatoes with 2 teaspoons of garlic, a big splash of olive oil, basil, salt, and pepper. Place all the slices of bread on a cookie sheet and toast each side for about 2 to 3 minutes. In a miniature bowl, mix 1 teaspoon of minced garlic with a splash or two of olive oil. With a pastry brush, quickly paint the toast slices with the oil mixture on both sides, sprinkle lightly with sea salt and fresh grinds of pepper (optional). Then, bake another minute or two at 350 F. Remove from the oven and top each bread slice with the chopped tomatoes and basil mixture. Arrange on a plate and serve as an antipasto or along side slices of fresh mozzarella cheese and Italian olives.

Note: Bruschetta is an antipasto from Italy consisting of oven-grilled bread, rubbed with garlic and topped with olive oil and sea salt. Variations may include toppings of fresh tomato, basil, oregano, Mozzarella, Parmesan, and Prosciutto - which is an Italian dry-cured ham thinly sliced.

CHESTNUT FLOUR FLATBREAD ★
(Castagnaccio O Migliaccio)

Bro. Joseph
Serves 4 - 6

3 tablespoons of raisins
   plumped in warm milk (below)
½ cup warm milk
1 tablespoon of sugar
1 pinch of salt
2 tablespoons of pignoli or
   walnuts chopped
2 cups milk
3 tablespoons olive oil

2 teaspoons rosemary, dried
   and crushed
1 teaspoon orange or almond
   extract
1 teaspoon baking powder
¼ all purpose flour
2 cups chestnut flour
Sea salt or Kosher rock salt
   (optional)

Preheat oven to 350 F. In a large mixing bowl, stir raisins, warm milk, sugar, plus 2 cups of milk, nuts, orange or almond extract and pinch of salt. Now, with a wooden spoon, stir in chestnut flour, all purpose flour, and baking powder to form a thick brownie-type batter. Pam spray a cast iron frying pan or 9-inch cake pan. Pour batter in the pan. Sprinkle the top with crushed dried rosemary, drizzles of olive oil and nuts (rock salt optional). Bake 30 to 40 minutes until toothpick comes out clean. Let stand 10 minutes, remove, and place on wire rack. Do not refrigerate. Serve at room temperature as a snack or with soup and salad. This recipe can be made gluten-free by removing the all purpose flour and adding more chestnut flour.

Note: Castagnaccio is a flatbread pizza that's been sold by street vendors in Rome, Italy for more than a thousand years. The original recipe is still available in ancient Roman cookbooks and was first found in 1993, while visiting the New York Public Library.

CINNAMON ROLLS
(Sunday Brunch Cinnabons)

Linda Grappo
Serves 6 - 8

2 packages of yeast
1 tablespoon sugar
1 cup lukewarm water
1 cup warm milk
6 tablespoons Crisco
½ cup sugar

2 teaspoons salt
7 cups flour
3 eggs beaten
6 tablespoons butter melted
1.5 cups brown sugar
1 tablespoon cinnamon

Dissolve yeast and 1 tablespoon sugar in lukewarm water. Add milk, shortening, sugar, and salt. Add 2 cups flour and eggs, beat well. Add remaining flour—enough to make a soft dough. (I use all 7 cups) Knead lightly and place in a greased bowl. Cover and set in a warm place and let rise until double—about 2 hours. (I use a dough hook attachment and knead dough in mixing bowl about 7 minutes or so at medium speed). Punch down and divide into 2 portions. Roll out into oblong pieces, ¼-inch thick. Brush with melted butter and sprinkle with brown sugar and cinnamon mixture. Roll up for jelly roll and cut into 1-inch slices. Place cut side up, about an inch apart, in large shallow greased baking pans. Cover and let rise in a warm place for about 1 hour. Bake at 350 F for about 20 to 30 minutes until golden brown. (Oven temp. and times will vary—watch after 20 minutes.) Makes about 2 to 4 dozen, depending on size. Ice while still warm. Simple glaze...powdered sugar, warm water, and vanilla extract. No exact measure...adjust to how thick or thin you want it, and your desired amount of vanilla extract.

COLORFUL CRANBERRY CHRISTMAS BREAD
(Quick Bread)

Bro. Joseph
Makes 2 Loaves

4 cups flour
2 cups sugar or 1.5 cups Truvia Sugar Blend
3 teaspoons baking powder
1 teaspoon baking soda
½ cup butter or canola oil
1.5 cups orange juice
2 tablespoons orange rind finely grated
2 eggs beaten
2 cups walnuts chopped
4 cups fresh cranberries lightly chopped

Preheat oven to 350 F. Use non-stick cooking spray on the bottom and sides of two bread loaf pans. Combine wet ingredients. On low-speed with an electric mixer or by hand, mix until well blended. Add dry ingredients and mix well. Fold in walnuts and cranberries by hand. Divide in half between two loaf pans. Bake for one hour and 10 minutes (until brown) and toothpick comes out clean. Cool completely to room temperature before slicing.

Note: A great way to add color and flavor to a festive Thanksgiving or Christmas holiday table.

CORN BREAD
(Award Winning)

Bro. Joseph
Serves 4 - 6

1¾ cups flour
1 cup cornmeal, white or yellow
1.5 cups sugar
½ teaspoon baking soda
½ teaspoon baking powder
½ teaspoon salt
3 large eggs slightly beaten
1.5 cups buttermilk or milk with 1.5 tablespoons of vinegar
1 teaspoon vanilla
½ cup melted Crisco
1 half can cream corn or 1 small can

Preheat oven to 375 F. Pam spray 9" x 13" glass baking dish. In a large mixing bowl, combine all dry ingredients. In another mixing bowl, combine all wet ingredients and mix well. Combine both mixtures with an electric mixer also adding the melted Crisco and creamed corn. Pour batter into the baking dish and place in oven for 30 minutes or until toothpick comes out clean and it's golden brown on top. In the springtime, for a creative touch add 1 tablespoon of finely grated orange or lemon rind to the batter. Goes great with Easter ham.

EASTER BREAD 🌐
(Pane Pasquale Italiano da Abruzzo)

Grandma Grappo
Makes 12 Large or 18 Medium Loaves

2 cups potatoes mashed
2 cups butter or margarine
2 cups eggs (about 15)
5 lbs. flour
6 packs Fleischman's Rapid Rise Yeast
10 teaspoons of Anise extract (or more to taste)

1.5 cups sugar
1 cup warm water, 100 degrees F.
6 drops yellow food coloring
1 tablespoon salt

Using your Kitchen Aid Mixer, combine butter by cutting into ¼ inch slices. Salt and flour mixing with the paddle attachment until it forms a grainy sand texture. In a small bowl combine the yeast, warm water, and sugar—stirring until dissolved and then set aside until foam forms. Meanwhile, in a large mixing bowl, whisk eggs, mashed potatoes, food coloring, and anise extract. Now, gradually combine the wet and dry ingredients by hand forming a smooth, soft dough ball. Remove from the bowl and layout the ball on a board and rest 2 minutes. Now, by hand knead the dough for 5 minutes and add additional flour as necessary so that it does not stick to the flour board. Place in a clean, dry, ungreased bowl—covered with a cloth—for one hour in a draft-free place. Take out and place on the bread board, and knead for one minute to redistribute the yeast. Cut into 12 equal pieces and form 12 loaves of bread. Bake in Pam spray loaf pans or Pam spray cookie sheets by braiding the dough with a simple, single braid, double braid or triple braid. Before placing in the oven, brush each one with a mixture of egg yolk and a tad of water. Bake 20 to 30 minutes at 325 F until brown and taps hollow. Remove and set on wire racks to cool. (There are many decorative variations to Italian Easter Bread Recipes. You can see how to make and decorate with Easter eggs by going to YouTube and watching someone make this recipe. You can also learn about braiding dough from some of these YouTube chefs.)

Note: In Italy, one well-loved Easter tradition is Pane di Pasqua, or Italian Easter Bread. This bread is fluffy and every so slightly sweet, flavored with light, springy flavors of citrus and anise. This particular recipe adds mashed potatoes, along with the springtime freshness of eggs. It adds texture, moisture and longevity to this bread. It will taste fresh for days!

EASTER BREAD 🌐
(Pane Pasquale Italiano da Calabria)

Grandma Sylvester
Makes 12 Large or 18 Medium Loaves

5 lbs. flour
15 eggs
5 teaspoons anise extract
3 tablespoons anise liquor
2 packs of Fleischman's Rapid Rise Yeast

1 tablespoon salt
1 cup sugar
½ cup canola oil
½ cup warm water, 100 degrees F
6 drops yellow food coloring

Dissolve yeast in small bowl with ½ cup warm water and 1 teaspoon of sugar. Stir until dissolved and set aside until it forms a foam, about 10 minutes. Have the eggs come to room temperature. In a large mixing bowl, whisk the eggs, anise, liquor and salt together. Next, whisk in the food coloring, oil, yeast, and sugar. Lastly, add the flour by hand until forming a soft ball. Remove—place on a bread board and let rest 2 minutes. Now knead by hand for 5 minutes, adding flour when necessary to make the dough smooth and not sticky. Cover and set the dough aside in a clean bowl and draft-free area for one hour. Punch the dough down and knead in the bowl for one minute to redistribute the yeast. Place on bread board and cut unto 12 equal pieces. Form into loaves, Pam spray loaf pans, or Pam spray cookie sheets forming the dough into braids, single, double or triple. Brush with mixture of egg yolk and tad of water, cover, and let rise for 20 minutes. Bake at 325 F for 20 to 25 minutes, or until brown and taps hollow. Remove from the oven and place on cooling racks.

Note: There are many decorative variations to Italian Easter Bread Recipes. You can see how to make and decorate with Easter eggs by going to YouTube and watching someone make this recipe. You can also learn about braiding dough from some of these YouTube chefs.

EGG TOAST ⊙
(Hole-in-the-Bread)

Bro. Joseph

4 eggs
4 pieces of sliced bread

Salt and pepper
2 pads of butter

Melt butter in a nonstick skillet on medium-high heat. Using a knife and cutting board, quickly cut a hole in the middle of each slice of bread. Place each slice of bread in the skillet adding one egg and seasonings to each hole. Then, brown bottom side for 2 to 3 minutes and top side 1 to 2 minutes. Serve for breakfast or dinner. Also, serve plain or sprinkled with cheese, bacon or ham bits—along with a side of jam or marmalade. Note, bread may be substituted with half of a bagel, also with a hole cut in the middle.

Note: Also known as egg-in-a-basket or egg-in-a-hole, it has been loved by families and campers in the United States since the late 1800s. An official recipe naming it "egg with a hat" first made an appearance in the Boston Cooking School Cookbook by Fannie Farmer in the 1890s, calling for a two-and-a-half-inch cookie cutter to remove the bread's center, which was served atop!

FRENCH TOAST ⊙
(Vanilla Pain Perdu)

Bro. Joseph
Serves 4

1 loaf of day-old American white bread or French bread, cut into slices
4 large eggs
2 tablespoons sugar

2 teaspoons pure vanilla extract
½ cup milk
½ cup almonds or pecans chopped

In a medium bowl, whisk eggs, sugar, vanilla, and milk to form a batter. In a large nonstick skillet, baste the bottom with a few drops of vegetable oil. Get the skillet hot on medium heat. Then, dip the bread on both sides in the batter and fry in the skillet. Flip sides once light brown on the bottom. Serve with butter, maple syrup, and garnish of chopped almonds or pecans.

Note: In America we call it "French Toast." In France the name of this dish is "Lost Bread" or "Pain Perdu." When translated it roughly means "Day-Old-Bread," dipped in egg and fried. In Belgium and France, Pain Perdu is often served for dinner with a side of split-pea soup.

FRIED DOUGH FEAST OF ST. JOSEPH 🎉
(Zeppole di San Giuseppe)

Paula Grappo
Serves 4 - 6

1 basic bread recipe	1 meat platter covered with paper towels
1 medium sauce pot ½ full canola oil	1 soup bowl of sugar or cinnamon sugar
1 slotted spoon	

Heat oil on medium-high heat until hot. You can test the temperature by dropping in a tiny piece of dough. Once dough starts to sizzle, it's time to make the Zeppole. Take your risen dough, deflate it, and knead it in the same bowl for a minute to redistribute the yeast. With a sharp knife, cut off pieces of dough and form into small balls, pillows, strips, and ties. Drop in the hot oil and occasionally (and carefully) flip over to brown on both sides. Remove with slotted spoon and place on paper towels. After a minute or so, dredge in the sugar bowl on both sides and serve. Although this is entertaining to children, remember to keep little ones far, far away from the stove when working with hot oil. They should be safe-seated at the kitchen table waiting for the first Zeppole to be served. Enjoy!

Note: Zeppole di San Giuseppe, a fried dough specialty made for the festival of St. Joseph from Enna, Sicily are loved throughout southern Italy. They are heavily associated with the same festival in Naples as well. The origin of zeppole, or zippula in Sicilian, comes from the Arabic zalbiyya, meaning fried soft dough. Paula fried a few of these whenever she made Italian bread.

ZUCCHINI BREAD ⊗
(Quick Bread)

Mary Lou Andrus
Serves 4

- 3 eggs
- 3 cups flour
- 1 cup oil
- 1 teaspoon salt
- 2 cups sugar or 1 ¼ cup Truvia Sugar Blend
- 1 teaspoon baking soda
- ½ teaspoon baking powder
- 1 teaspoon pure vanilla extract (not imitation)
- ½ cup walnuts or pecans chopped
- 2 cups zucchini, shredded on the wide-hole cheese grater

In a mixer, beat eggs slightly and then add oil, sugar, and vanilla—mix well. With a paddle attachment or by hand, add zucchini, dry ingredients, and nuts. Mix well. Pour into 2 Pam sprayed loaf pans and bake at 325 F for 60-75 minutes. Check after 60 minutes with toothpick. When fully baked, remove from the oven and place pans on wire rack. After completely cooled, place on serving dish and drizzle tops with powdered sugar and water glaze if desired.

Note: Also, for breakfast, lunch, or high tea (4 pm), slice the loaves and then cut each piece in half. Spread one half with a thick layer of whipped cream cheese (regular or strawberry) and then form a sandwich. Cut in half again and insert with a party toothpick through the middle. Great for holiday buffets and platters.

ZÜPFE SUISSE SUNDAY BREAD ✿
(Tresse Pain du Dimanche)

Esther Meirer
Serves 6 - 8

2 packs of fresh dry yeast or ½ a large cake of yeast
3 tablespoons sugar
½ cup butter softened
2 cups lukewarm milk
½ teaspoon of salt
4 cups bread flour
2 tablespoons vital wheat gluten

Early Sunday morning, make yourself a nice cup of coffee or tea and get ready to make Swiss Sunday Bread! Using an electric mixer, cream sugar, salt, butter, and yeast until whipped together like a butter cream frosting. Turn machine on low and, with the paddle attachment, add the lukewarm milk. Now, use the dough hook and add vital wheat gluten, along with the flour, until it forms a medium-soft ball. Now, Pam spray 2 cookie sheets—bottom and sides. On a kitchen counter or board, divide the dough into 3 equal parts. Form three loaves by using the simple braid method or four-string swiss braid method. (Examples are available on YouTube) Let rise covered for 45 to 60 minutes. Now brush the tops of the bread after whisking together a mixture of 2 egg yolks and a little bit of water. Immediately bake at 350 F for 40 to 45 minutes, until loaves tap hollow and are golden brown. Enjoy Swiss Sunday Bread with Kerrygold Irish Creamery Butter and Bonne Mama French country jams for an authentic European dining experience.

Note: Zopf or Züpfe is a type of Swiss, Austrian, or Bavarian bread made from white flour, milk, eggs, butter, and yeast. The dough is brushed with egg yolk before baking, lending it its golden crust. It is baked in the form of a braid and traditionally eaten on Sunday mornings. In 1976 Esther taught me her recipe one Sunday morning in her home in the German-speaking Swiss Alps.

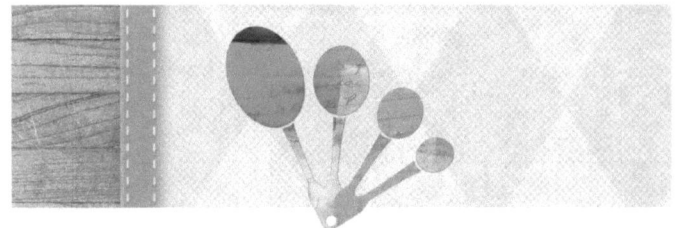

Desserts

DESSERTS

APPLE CAKE

Rosemary Allegretto
Serves 6 - 8

- 1½ cups lightly packed brown sugar or (1 cup Splenda Brown Sugar Blend)
- 1 cup canola oil
- 3 eggs slightly beaten
- 2 cups flour
- 1 heaping teaspoon cinnamon
- 1 teaspoon baking soda
- 1 teaspoon baking powder
- ½ cup walnuts or pecans chopped
- ¾ cup milk
- 3 medium to large baking apples peeled, cored, and sliced

Preheat oven to 350 F. In an electric mixer whip the sugar, oil, and three eggs for 5 minutes on high. In a medium bowl, sift the dry ingredients together. Blend into wet ingredients on low speed. Fold in the nuts and apples by hand. Place in a 9" x 13" glass baking dish (use non-stick cooking spray), bake for 30 to 35 minutes at 350 F. Use a toothpick to check when cake is done. (It should come out clean.) Cool to room temperature. Sprinkle with a strainer filled with 4 tablespoons of powdered sugar. Dust the top lightly and serve warm or at room temperature. Works well topped with hot Apple Chutney, Cool Whip, or a scoop of Ben & Jerry's vanilla ice cream.

Note: Take your family and friends apple picking in the fall and then make this cake to celebrate the season. Excellent eating and baking apples are: Braeburn, Cortland, Empire, Granny Smith, McIntosh, Rome, and Jonathan. In the 1970s, Rosemary Allegretto frequently made Apple Cake for our Friday night prayer group and it was always a hit!

APPLE CRISP ★
(All American Apple Crisp)

Karen Hoth
Serves 8 - 10

10 baking apples—peeled, cored, and sliced
¼ cup sugar
2 teaspoons of cinnamon
2 tablespoons of fresh or bottled lemon juice
¼ teaspoon nutmeg
1 cup butter melted
2 cups oatmeal
1 cup brown sugar or ½ cup Splenda Brown Sugar Blend
1 cup flour

Preheat oven to 350 F. In a large mixing bowl, place sliced apples and lemon juice. Toss with ¼ cup sugar, cinnamon and nutmeg. Set aside and let rest. Topping: In a separate medium-sized bowl combine the butter, oatmeal, brown sugar, and flour. Pam spray a 9" x 13" glass dish and line the bottom with the apple mixture. Lastly spread topping over the apples. Bake for 30 to 45 minutes, or until golden brown.

Note: Karen is the wife of a Continental Airlines mechanic, Daryl Hoth, who was working at LAX for many years. She introduced this recipe while on a church camping trip to Lake Elsinore in 1975. Everyone loved it!

BANANAS FOSTER 🌎
(Bananas in Dark Rum Sauce)

Chef Yves
Serves 4 - 6

6 firm bananas
2 tablespoons butter
½ cup dark rum
2 limes

Melt butter in a nonstick frying pan. Add sugar and caramelize to a light brown color on medium-high. Place bananas cut in ½ lengthwise. Brown on both sides. Add rum. Now, carefully flambé (ignite) the rum and allow the flame to go out naturally. All the while shake the pan back and forth to deglaze the contents with the juice of two limes. Reduce for 1 to 2 minutes more, (meaning until it forms a saucy glaze over the bananas). Serve hot with a garnish of Ben & Jerry's Chunky Monkey Ice Cream and mint leaf on top.

Note: Bananas Foster... In the early 1950s, New Orleans was the major port of entry for bananas being shipped from Central and South America. Owen Brennan, owner of Brennan's Restaurant, challenged his chef, Paul Blange, to include bananas in a new dessert. The rest is history, Bananas Foster was born!

BLUEBERRY COFFEE CAKE ⊗

Bro. Joseph
Serves 6 - 8

1 cup butter
2 cups sugar
6 eggs lightly beaten
2 teaspoons baking soda
½ teaspoon salt
2 teaspoons baking powder
4 cups flour
2 cups sour cream

4 cups blueberries, fresh or frozen
TOPPING
2 cups brown sugar
½ cup butter
1/ cup flour
1 tablespoon cinnamon (optional)

Preheat oven to 350 F. Using a Kitchen Aid Mixer, cream sugar and butter until smooth. Add eggs until batter forms and then add vanilla and sour cream. In a small bowl, have ready a mixture of flour, baking powder, baking soda, and salt. Slowly incorporate the dry ingredients into the wet ingredients. Turn the machine off and gently fold the blueberries in by hand with a spatula. Pam spray a 9" x 13" glass baking dish and pour it into the blueberry batter. Next, have your topping ready in a small bowl by combining with a fork the brown sugar, butter, (optional cinnamon), and flour to form grainy sprinkles over the top. Bake for 30 to 35 minutes—or until a toothpick inserted in the middle comes out clean.

Note: This blueberry coffee cake has its origins in Polish, Croatian, and Slovakian cooking where sour cream is often used in their cuisine. Enjoy the taste of Eastern Europe!

CHEESE CAKE 🎀
(Award Winning Cheese Cake)

Paul Grappo
Serves 8

10 sheets of graham cracker squares
2 tablespoons butter melted
2 tablespoons sugar
Filling
2 8-oz. packs of cream cheese softened
1 cup sugar
1 pint sour cream
3 eggs room temperature
2 teaspoons vanilla extract
1 can Comstock or Thank You Brand Blueberry or Cherry Pie Topping

Preheat oven to 350 F. First make the pie crust. In a medium bowl crush the graham crackers finely. Blend with margarine and sugar. Spread on a Pam spray deep 9" inch pie dish. Set aside. In an electric mixer beat cream cheese, eggs, vanilla, and sugar. Once creamy, turn off the mixer and fold in the sour cream with a spatula. Pour batter over crust and bake for 30 minutes. Now, turn oven off. DO NOT OPEN! Let rest in oven for 60 minutes. Then, remove from oven and run a sharp knife around it to loosen the sides. Then, gently match up your cake dish to the top and carefully flip over. Graham cracker crust is not on top. Let cool. Before serving top with blueberry or cherry pie filling.

Note: Whether it was Thanksgiving, Christmas, or Easter, Paula won many accolades over decades for this recipe from family, friends, and the "church ladies." The recipe was never shared with anyone until now!

CHERRIES JUBILEE ☺

Angela Chavez
Serves 4 - 6

1 16-oz. tub sour cream
1 large box Jell-O Vanilla Instant Pudding
2 cans Comstock or Thank You brand cherry pie filling
1 Pillsbury Angel Food Cake made according to directions

Make the vanilla pudding as directed on the box. Once it is set, fold in the sour cream by hand and then set aside. Once the cake cools completely, cut into squares. Using a tall clear glass salad or punch bowl, build layers of cake beginning at the bottom, alternating vanilla cream and cherry glaze. Repeat the layers. Cover with plastic wrap and chill before serving.

CHERRY TORTE 🎀

Paula Grappo
Serves 6 - 8

6 egg whites beaten stiffly
¾ teaspoon cream of tartar, beaten into egg whites
¾ cup of sugar
2 teaspoons of vanilla
2 cups Saltine crackers (No salt - but you can also rub the salt off if you do not have salt free crackers)
¾ cups pecans or walnuts chopped
2 large tubs of regular or sugar free Cool Whip
2 cans of Thank You Brand or Comstock Cherry Filling

After beating the eggs and cream of tartar into stiff peaks, slowly add sugar and vanilla while beating at high speed. Now, turn off the machine and fold the crackers and nuts in by hand using a wooden spoon. Spray Pam on a 9" x 13" glass dish, pour mixture onto bottom, and spread evenly. Bake for 25 minutes in a 350 F preheated oven. Remove from oven and cool completely on a wire rack. Once cold, spread Cool Whip over the crust. Carefully spread the 2 cans of cherries over the top the Cool Whip. Try not to disturb the whipped topping on the bottom. Cover with cellophane and refrigerate 3 to 4 hours or overnight. It will keep for 3 to 4 days.

Note: For decades, Paula received rave reviews for Cherry Torte from guests, family, church ladies, and at all the potlucks and picnics. Cherry Torte is also colorfully red, and perfectly festive for holidays, Christmas Day and birthdays!

CHOCOLATE GERMAN BLACK FOREST CAKE ⊗
(Schwarzwderkirschtorte)

Bro. Joseph
Serves 6

1 Betty Crocker German Chocolate or Double Chocolate cake mix
1 can Comstock or Thank You brand Cherry Filling
1 tub Pillsbury German Chocolate Frosting with pecans and coconut or Pillsbury Chocolate Frosting
1 can Pam spray

Bake the cake in two nonstick round pans, according to recipe. Be sure to spray Pam heavily on the bottom and crease area of the pans. Let cakes cool to room temperature. Next, with a knife, loosen the edges of the cake and flip onto center of cake dish. Spread the cherry filling across the first layer. Now do the same with the second layer, loosen with a knife, and flip onto the center of the cake dish, flat side down and lightly sink it into the cherry filling. Lastly, ice the top of the cake with German Chocolate Pecan-Coconut Icing or Double Chocolate Icing. Icing the sides is not necessary if you have cherry filling pouring out from the sides. Decorate the top with chocolate sprinkles and Maraschino Cherries. You may wish to serve each cake slice with a garnish of homemade Creme Fraiche, Reddi-Wip, vanilla ice cream, or Cool Whip.

Note: Black Forest cakes are attributed to several German pastry chefs, including Josef Keller of the Café Ahrend in Bad Godesberg in 1915. It began appearing in the United States in the early 1960s. Unlike most European cakes, Black Forest was widely adopted by Americans. The confection eventually made its way into bakeries and upscale restaurants, as well home kitchens.

ITALIAN RICOTTA CAKE ⊘
(Quick and Easy Springtime Cake)

Bro. Joseph
Serves 6 - 8

1 box yellow cake mix, made according to instructions
2 lbs. tub of Ricotta Cheese
¾ cup sugar
4 eggs beaten on high for two minutes
½ teaspoon vanilla

Have ready a 9" x 13" glass baking dish sprayed with Pam. Pour cake mix into the baking dish. In a separate bowl, mix together the Ricotta, sugar, eggs, and vanilla. Pour the mixture over the cake batter and bake at 350 F for 35 to 45 minutes or until toothpick comes out clean. Cool and dust top with powdered sugar. Garnish slices before serving with whipped topping and a fresh strawberry. Cake tastes best slightly warm or at room temperature.

Note: Italian cooking has included the now popular cheesecake as a staple since Roman times. Cato the Elder, in 160 BC, included two cheesecake recipes in his writings that were recommended for religious festivals and dinners.

JELL-O POKE CAKE ✣
(Cool Whip Vanilla Pudding Topping)

Bro. Joseph
Serves 4 - 6

- 1 box white or yellow cake, made according to directions
- 1 Jell-O Sugar-free 3 oz. packet of strawberry or raspberry
- 1 Jell-O Instant Vanilla Pudding 3 oz. whisk with 1 cup milk and ¼ cup powdered sugar
- 1 Cool Whip sugar-free or low-fat

Let cake cool for 20 minutes or more. Prepare Jell-O with 1 cup boiling water, ½ cup cold water, and 3 oz. strawberry or raspberry packet. Using the end of a wood mixing spoon, poke holes evenly all over the cake. Pour Jell-O mixture all over the cake—especially filling the holes. Cover and place in refrigerator—level on a rack overnight. The next day, right before serving, it's optional to cover the top of the cake with fresh-sliced strawberries. Set aside and make the frosting: In a mixing bowl, put the package of Jell-O Instant Vanilla Pudding and whisk in 1 cup milk and 1/4 cup powdered sugar. Once it sets (about 8 minutes), fold in with a spatula 8 oz. Cool Whip Topping. Spread over the top of the cake and serve.

Note: Poke cakes are kitschy and dated, but still a lot of fun for everyone. Poke cakes go back to the ancient days of the 1970s when housewives had to host many dinner parties and entertain many a working man's bosses. Serving this cake, she was considered the "hostess with the mostess!"

JELLY ROLL CAKE ★
(Torta Viana)

Isabel Silva
Serves 6 - 8

2 cups sugar
2 cups flour
7 eggs

½ cup orange juice
1 tablespoon baking powder

Preheat oven to 350 F. Using an electric mixer, whip all ingredients on medium speed for 3 minutes. Heavily Pam spray a large cookie sheet. Pour batter into the cookie sheet and bake for 20 to 25 minutes until lightly brown and toothpick comes out clean. Next, cool on a wire rack for 30 minutes. Then, take a large kitchen towel, lightly wet it and coat the top of the towel with sugar. Flip the cookie sheet cake onto the wet towel. Once out (tap pan with a butter knife all over if necessary), lather the cake with your favorite store-bought or homemade berry jam. Roll and place crease down on a cake serving plate. Dust with powdered sugar in a hand strainer. Makes a beautiful presentation for the Christmas holidays with the "snow," red berry center, and a garnish of fresh green mint leaves.

Note: Isabel (Viana is her nickname) who is from Spain, received accolades from everyone (including her son, Joey) whenever she made this wonderful jelly roll infused with European pastry flair and lots of love.

PECAN CRUNCH
(Pistachio Pudding Dessert)

Angela Chavez
Serves 8 - 10

Crust
1 cup flour
1 stick butter softened
½ cup pecans chopped
Filling
1 8-oz. package cream cheese
softened
1 cup powdered sugar
2 tablespoons sour cream
(optional)
1 large tub of Cool Whip
2 small packs instant pistachio
pudding, make according to
directions, let set to gel

Preheat oven to 350 F. In a mixing bowl, combine the flour, pecans, and butter to form a dry mix. Then, pat the mixture on the bottom of a 9" x 13" glass baking dish. Bake for 15 minutes. Remove, cool, and set aside. Next, with an electric mixer, whip together the cream cheese, powdered sugar, and sour cream (optional). Remove the beaters, scrape into bowl and, using a spatula, gently fold in with one cup of Cool Whip. Now, spread that over the cooled crust. Next, pour the prepared instant pistachio pudding over the first layer. Lastly, spread the remainder of the Cool Whip over the top. Sprinkle more chopped pecans before serving. Chill for at least one hour—or you can make the dessert the night before. Enjoy!

Note: Angela was given this recipe from her mom in 1978 and it has been a hit among family and friends ever since.

PINEAPPLE UPSIDE-DOWN CAKE

Bro. Joseph
Serves 6 - 8
Makes two cake pans 8 - 9 inches round

1 Pillsbury Yellow Cake, made according to directions
½ cup butter melted
1 cup brown sugar
2 large cans pineapple slices
14 maraschino cherries

Preheat oven to 350 F. Make yellow cake and set aside. Pam spray two cake pans 8 to 9 inches round. Place melted butter and brown sugar in each pan and blend with a spatula. Place the pineapple slices on the bottom of both pans and one cherry in the middle of each slice of pineapple. Pour ½ the cake batter in each pan. Bake for 40 to 45 minutes until brown and toothpick comes out of the center clean. Remove from the oven and cool on a wire rack for 10 minutes. Invert onto a cake dish. Serve warm with Cool Whip, whipped cream, or vanilla ice cream.

Note: The History of Pineapple Upside-down Cake: The idea of cooking a cake upside down is an old technique that started centuries ago when cakes were cooked in cast iron skillets. It was easy to add fruit and sugar in the bottom of the pan and a simple cake batter on top and put it over the fire to cook. By 1923, it was being referred to in magazines and cookbooks as such.

RASPBERRY SAUCE
(Sauce aux Framboises)

Bro. Joseph

3½ cups raspberries, fresh or frozen
2 cups powdered sugar
1 tablespoon fresh-strained or bottled lemon juice
1 tablespoon water

In a medium saucepan, over moderate heat, stir together raspberries, water, powdered sugar, and lemon juice. Heat, stirring often, until raspberries begin to soften. Raise heat to moderately high and simmer, stirring occasionally, until slightly thickened, about 2-3 minutes. Strain through a fine strainer or pour into cheese cloth once cool and squeeze into a small bowl. Throw away seeds and debris. (Sauce can be made ahead and refrigerated, covered, up to 1 week.) Hint: Make a fresh raspberry vinaigrette dressing for a leafy green salad by whisking 1 cup of raspberry sauce with ⅛ cup Balsamic vinegar, ¼ cup olive oil, salt and pepper to taste.

Note: Serve the raspberry sauce warm over your favorite vanilla or chocolate ice cream, topped with your favorite gourmet biscuit cookie (In Europe - "Coupe Denmark"). Adds a colorful and excellent ending to a wonderful holiday meal. Also, try warm raspberry sauce on grilled meats and cold raspberry sauce is tasty under or over cheesecake slices from the bakery or freezer case.

RICOTTA PIE ✿
(Italian Ricotta Easter Pie)

Lena Grappo
Serves 4 - 6

1 ¼ pound tub of Ricotta cheese
1 tablespoon white or regular raisins
1 pinch of salt
2 teaspoons orange rind grated, fine side of a cheese grater
1 tablespoon flour

2 egg whites beaten stiff
4 tablespoons sugar
2 tablespoons confectioners sugar
4 egg yolks
1 teaspoon cinnamon

Preheat oven to 375 F. Next, blend with an electric mixer for 5 minutes the ricotta, salt, flour, sugar, egg yolks, and orange rind. On slow-speed, add raisins and orange peel. Lastly, fold in gently the beaten egg whites with a wooden spoon. Pam spray very well an 8 or 9 inch round cake pan. Pour in the batter and bake for 35 minutes or until firm. Remove from oven, let cool on a wire rack, run knife around the edges and flip onto a serving dish. Once completely cool, sprinkle from a hand strainer a dusting of confectioners sugar blended with cinnamon.

Note: Italian Ricotta Pie is popular any time of year, but a specialty at Easter time. It's often served at springtime family gatherings, St. Joseph's Table, and as a dessert alongside ham and pineapple stuffing dinners and family buffets.

SPANISH SPICE BAR CAKE 🎀
(The Original A & P Spanish Spice Bar Cake)

Bro. Joseph
Serves 4 - 6

2 cups flour
1.5 cups sugar
1.5 teaspoons baking soda
1 tablespoon cocoa powder
1 teaspoon cinnamon
1 teaspoon salt
1 teaspoon nutmeg
1 teaspoon allspice
½ cup canola oil
2 cups applesauce
2 medium eggs slightly beaten
1 cup raisins, plumped in warm water 10 minutes and drained

Frosting
1 8-oz. package cream cheese softened
4 tablespoons butter softened
2 teaspoons vanilla extract
1.5 cups powdered sugar
¼ cup milk (Add teaspoons more if needed)
1 tablespoon fresh or bottled lemon juice

Preheat oven to 350 F. Pam spray well a 9" x 13" glass baking dish. In a large bowl, sift together your spices, cocoa, salt, and the other dry ingredients. Next, add the vegetable oil, applesauce, and the beaten eggs. When all of the above is mixed, add the plumped raisins. Put in the cake pan and bake for 30 to 35 minutes. Frosting: Using an electric mixer, blend the cream cheese, butter, vanilla, confectioners sugar, milk, and lemon juice together. To make a layer cake, just like the original Spanish Bar Cake, cut the cake down the middle into 2 pieces. Then, spread the frosting between the layers, stack, and icing on the top. Step back in time and enjoy this great cake!

Note: A blast from the past, think 1960s and S & H Green Stamps. The beloved A & P Spanish Spice Cake immortalizes America's postwar generations that shopped at the Great Atlantic and Pacific Tea Company!

Cookies & Candy

COOKIES & CANDY

BISCOTTI
(Italian Biscotti Cookies)

Bro. Joseph
Makes 100 Cookies

1 lb. butter lightly softened
2 cups sugar or 1.5 cups Truvia Blend Sugar
6 eggs beaten
1.5 tablespoons pure Anise extract
8 cups flour
3 tablespoons baking powder
1 box confectioners powdered sugar
1 box food coloring
Holiday sprinkles

Preheat oven to 350 F. Lightly soften butter. Then, whip with eggs and sugar using the paddle in the electric mixer. Add anise. In a separate bowl, stir together the flour and baking powder. Slowly add to butter mixture on low speed. Make into soft dough. Shape into U, S, O pillows. Bake 20 minutes on a lightly greased cookie sheet until light brown. Cool to room temperature. Make a lightly smooth confectioners glaze of powdered sugar and water. Color glaze in separate bowls with red, green, or other colors. Sprinkle with Christmas sprinkles (optional) while the glaze is still wet.

Note: These cookies are great for Christmas and Easter, but also for anniversaries and weddings—simply by changing the glaze colors to white or pastels, then add silver, gold, white, or pastel sprinkles.

CHOCOLATE COVERED STRAWBERRIES

Bro. Joseph
Serves 6 - 8

2 16-oz. bags chocolate chips
1 8-oz. bag white chocolate chips
5 tablespoons Crisco
1 set double boiler
4 cookie sheets
1 roll wax paper
2 pounds very fresh strawberries with green leaves

Triple wash the strawberries in cold water and pat each one dry. Set aside. Melt in a double boiler (warm water to low simmer) 2 bags of chocolate chips, adding 2 to 4 tablespoons of Crisco as needed to thin out the chocolate for easy dipping. Do not add milk or water, it will turn the chocolate to dry paste. Stir the chocolate with a wooden spoon in double boiler until creamy smooth. Remove from stove top, dip strawberries in the chocolate, and line up one inch apart on wax paper lined cookie sheet. Set aside. Clean double boiler well with soap and water. Now, repeat with white chocolate chips, adding 1 to 2 tablespoons of Crisco as needed to make it smooth and creamy. Remove from heat and use a fork or teaspoon to drizzle decorative thin streams of white chocolate over the strawberries. Be careful, don't hit the green leaves with white or dark chocolate or they will shrivel and die. Refrigerate and serve within 24 hours (maximum).

Note: Besides Christmas and Easter, these are perfect for weddings when decorated with bow ties, bells, butterflies, roses, and more.

CHOCOLATE FUDGE ♪
(Christmas Fudge Squares)

Bro. Joseph
Serves 8 - 10

1.5 sticks of butter
3 cups sugar
1 5-oz. can evaporated milk
1 12-oz. bag semisweet
   chocolate chips

1 cup walnuts or pecans
   chopped
1 teaspoon vanilla
1 7-oz. jar marshmallow cream

Pam spray a 13" x 9" glass baking dish. In a sauce pan, mix butter, sugar, and milk. Bring to a boil within 5 minutes on medium heat. Candy thermometer should reach 234 degrees F. Remove sauce pan from the heat and fold in the chocolate chips with a wooden spoon until melted. Now fold in the vanilla, nuts, and lastly the marshmallow cream. Spread in the glass baking dish evenly. Cool at room temperature for 2 to 3 hours. Cut into squares. Yes, this is the original Fantasy Fudge recipe from the back of the Kraft Marshmallow Creme jar. It's a tried and tested recipe, having many decades of success.

Note: There are variations to this recipe available online—ranging from using peanut butter in the mix to incorporating coconut, pistachios, or macadamia nuts.

CHOCOLATE NUT CLUSTERS ♪
(Homemade Chocolate Candy)

Bro. Gary Joseph
Serves 6 - 8

1 cup chocolate chips
1 tablespoon Crisco oil
Nuts

Christmas candy cup liners
   from Michael's Craft Store

Set aside the nuts you have chosen. Next, warm one bag of chocolate chips in a double boiler. Use Crisco if the glaze needs to be smoother. Stir in nuts with a wooden spoon. Make "Rocky Road Clusters" by allowing the mixture to cool slightly longer and then gently fold in miniature marshmallows. If adding marshmallows, cool the chocolate just until it can stir. Use a small ice cream scoop to fill each candy cup liner. It makes about two dozen. Chill in refrigerator until ready to serve. They make nice holiday gifts in Ball pint or quart jars with a ribbon.

COOKIES NO BAKE 🎵
(Stained Glass Cookies)

Mary D'Amico
Serves 20

4 cups chocolate chips, dark or milk chocolate	2 cups walnuts or pecans, chopped
1 cup butter	2 small bags of coconut
6 cups multicolor miniature marshmallows	1 roll of wax paper

Gently melt chocolate and butter in a double boiler over hot water. Cool about 4 minutes. Fold in the nuts, miniature marshmallows, along with one bag of coconut. With the other bag of coconut, sprinkle sheets of wax paper and spread the mixture over the sheet. Roll the mixture into a log and cool in the refrigerator for 3 to 4 hours or overnight. Cut into cookie slices when ready to serve.

Note: Aunt Mary made these no bake cookies as a Christmas tradition, year after year.

CRANBERRY PRESERVES 🎵
(Christmas Holidays Cranberry Preserves)

Bro. Joseph
Makes up to 12, 4 oz Canning Jars

2 12-oz bags fresh cranberries washed and picked over	1 cup orange juice
3 cups sugar	1 cup water
1 heaping teaspoon cinnamon	3 tablespoons finely grated zest of orange rind

Combine all ingredients in a medium sauce pan, simmer 20 minutes. Let cool, pulse in blender, leaving some chunks of cranberry. Pour into 1 case (a dozen) sterilized 4-oz. jelly jars, leaving ¼ inch from top. Seal and boil in water bath upside down for 5 minutes. Remove with tongs. Wait until tops pop. If they don't, they will need to be refrigerated. Serve at Thanksgiving and Christmas for breakfast on English Muffins, Irish Soda Bread, toast, or cranberry scones. Serve in a small bowl as a chutney for roasted duck, turkey, and chicken.

Note: Homemade cranberry preserves make a wonderful, tasty, and personalized Christmas gift by simply tying a ribbon around it and placing a bow on top. Nothing like cranberries to bring color, taste, and the old-world charm to the Christmas season!

CREAM PUFFS ★

Beverly Jean Grappo
Serves 4 - 6

½ cup butter softened
1 cup boiling water
1 cup flour
¼ teaspoon salt
4 eggs

Boil water and butter together. Remove from heat. With an electric mixer, blend in the salt and flour. Now, add one egg at a time until mixture becomes smooth. Grease a large cookie sheet with Pam spray. Drop the mixture by tablespoon 2 inches apart. Bake at 450 F for 10 minutes. Then, bake at 400 for 20 to 25 minutes. Cool completely on a wire rack. Slightly slit each cream puff with a knife. Fill with vanilla or chocolate, instant or cooked Jell-O pudding, or ice cream. Sprinkle tops with powdered sugar and serve. Or, you can ice tops with chocolate frosting and colorful sprinkles for festive occasions.

Note: Cream puffs are a French family aristocrat desserts. They debuted in the U.S. in the 1880s. The first cream puffs originated in France during the 1540's when Catherine de Medici's pastry chef created the baked puffed shells for Catherine's husband, Henry II of France. My sister Beverly, made this during football season and girls night sleepovers.

ICING BUTTERCREAM ❄
(CAKE FROSTING)

Donna Quinn
Makes One 9 x 13 Sheetcake
Makes Two 9 Inch Rounds

1 cup of pure egg whites (no yellows or shells)
2 cups sugar
2 lbs. unsalted sweet butter room temperature
1 teaspoon vanilla extract

In the top of a double boiler, using an electric mixer, whisk the egg whites until stiff. Then, add the sugar over the double boiler until melted and warm to touch. Now, place mixer on high speed and start adding room temperature butter. Don't rush the process; take your time. Add butter slowly and once it is all in, add the vanilla. At this point you can stop, or you can add embellishments to your buttercream—such as food coloring, melted white, milk chocolate, or dark chocolate morsels. You can also add Grand Manier or other liquors as you like. Note: buttercream frosting freezes well. It can stay refrigerated up to one week. To reconstitute, melt half of what you have in a microwave. In a mixer combine the melted with the frozen and whip on high speed. If it's too soft, refrigerate and whip again.

ICING CARAMEL FROSTING 🎀
(Cake Frosting for Carrot, Banana, and Spice Cakes)

Paula Grappo
Covers One 9 x 13 Sheet Cake
Covers two 9 inch round

1.5 cups brown sugar
¾ cup water
3 egg whites (no shells or yellow)

½ teaspoon cream of tartar
2 teaspoons vanilla
½ teaspoon lemon extract or concentrate

In a small saucepan, boil sugar and water until it forms a tea color and drops put in ice water form soft balls. This is called soft ball stage. Remove from heat and set aside to cool. Now, in an electric mixer, beat the egg whites until stiff peaks form. Add cream of tartar. Then, on high speed, drizzle in the syrup until fluffy icing forms. Now, add vanilla and lemon concentrate or extract.

Note: For decades, Paula always made birthday cakes with this frosting, it was the most requested, especially on banana cake.

ICING CREAMY WHITE 🎀
(Frosting for white cakes, strawberry, cherry, lemon and more!)

Paula Grappo
Covers one 9 x 13 Sheet Cake
Covers two 9-inch rounds

1.5 cups granulated white sugar
¾ cup water
3 egg whites (no shells or yellows)

½ teaspoon cream of tartar
2 teaspoons of vanilla

In a small saucepan, boil sugar and water until it forms a light tea color and drops put in ice water form soft balls. This is called soft ball stage. Remove from heat and set aside to cool. Now, in an electric mixer, beat the egg whites until stiff peaks form. Add cream of tartar. Then, on high speed, drizzle in the syrup until fluffy icing forms. Now add vanilla and whip.

Note: Paula's cooked frosting was always a hit at birthdays, weddings, and parties. Be sure to eat it all up the same day because meringue frostings begin to dissipate overnight.

ORIGINAL TOLL HOUSE COOKIES 🍪
(Nestle Toll House Chocolate Chip Cookies)

Paula Grappo
12 Large Cookies
24 Small Cookies

2.5 cups flour
1 teaspoon baking soda
2 sticks butter
1 ⅓ cups brown sugar or ¾ cup Splenda Brown Sugar Blend
2 extra large eggs
2 teaspoons vanilla extract
1 teaspoon sea salt
1 lb. chocolate disks coarsely chopped or 1 bag large chocolate chips

1. Heat the oven to 325 F. 2. In a medium bowl, sift together the flour and baking soda. Set aside. 3. In the bowl of a stand mixer, fitted with the paddle attachment, or in a large bowl using a hand mixer, cream together the butter, brown sugar, and granulated sugar until light and fluffy. 4. Add the eggs, beating them in one at a time, until completely incorporated, then beat in the vanilla. 5. Add the flour mixture, then the salt, and mix until completely combined to form the dough. Fold in the chocolate pieces with the machine paddle turning slowly or by hand. 6. Scoop a generous heaping tablespoon of the mixture for each cookie, spacing them wide apart on parchment-lined baking sheets. Be sure to leave enough space as the cookies will spread, placing no more than 3 cookies across on each sheet. 7. Bake the cookies until set and lightly browned on the edges, 16 to 20 minutes. Remove and place the baking sheet on a rack until the cookies are cooled (Snitching 1 or 2 is ok). Repeat until all the cookie dough is gone. Adding chopped walnuts (optional). At Christmastime, try dusting the tops with a strainer filled with 2 tablespoons of powdered sugar before serving!

Note: Ruth, a Northeast inn owner, struck a 1930s deal with Nestle. A lifetime supply of chocolate chips in exchange for her recipe printed on the back of each chocolate chip bag. Ruth died in 1977, and the Toll House Inn burned down from a fire that started in the kitchen on New Year's Eve 1984. The inn was never rebuilt.

SNOWBALL COOKIES ❄
(Wedding Cookies)

Paula Grappo
Serves 20

1 cup butter
⅔ cup powdered sugar
2 tablespoons water
1 tablespoon vanilla

2.5 cups flour
1 cup chopped pecans or walnuts
1 dash of salt

Preheat oven to 350 F. Lightly soften butter and cream with powdered sugar. Add vanilla. Gently work in all the other ingredients. Roll by hand into miniature snowballs and place on a lightly greased cookie sheet an inch apart. Bake for 20 to 25 minutes or until tops and bottoms are a light golden brown. Remove from oven and leave on cookie sheet to cool on a wire rack. Chill completely to room temperature before touching—and then dredge in powdered sugar. Wait one hour and coat again in powdered sugar. They freeze well ahead of time in one- quart slider bags, thaw on a tray and then use powdered sugar right before a holiday party.

Note: Paula made this cookie an annual Christmas tradition, as well as a special treat for weddings, anniversaries, and family gatherings.

STRAWBERRY FREEZER JAM ❄

Bro. Joseph
Makes 18 Small Jelly Jars

3 quarts fresh strawberries, washed and sliced
6 tablespoons fresh or bottled lemon concentrate
10 cups sugar

2¼ cups water
3 boxes fruit pectin (49g each)
18 small jelly jars or 9 pint canning jars

Place the sliced strawberries in a large mixing bowl—tossing with lemon juice and sugar. Let rest for ten minutes. In a saucepan, combine water and pectin and bring to a boil. Pour the mixture over the strawberries and gently stir. Ladle into clean jars leaving ½ inch room at the top for freezer expansion. Now place in the freezer for one year or refrigerator for 3 to 4 weeks.

Note: This strawberry freezer jam is super easy to make, incredibly sweet, and tasty like no other strawberry jam! The key is that the strawberries aren't cooked—so they taste amazing and fresh. This has been a southern tradition for centuries.

Parties, Picnics & Family Gatherings

PARTIES, PICNICS & FAMILY GATHERINGS

BARBECUED CHICKEN ✚
(Barbecued Chicken with Homemade Barbecue Sauce)

Jane Motzinger
Serves 6 - 8

5 lbs. chicken parts
1 egg well beaten
1 cup apple cider vinegar
1 tablespoon salt
¼ teaspoon pepper
1 small onion finely chopped
2 teaspoons fresh parsley minced
½ teaspoon celery salt
½ teaspoon dried or fresh tarragon
½ teaspoon dried or fresh thyme

Grill chicken for 24 minutes, browning each side for 12 minutes with onion salt, garlic salt, and black pepper. Meanwhile, place all the other ingredients in a blender and pulse for 5 seconds. Then, pour into a sauce bowl with a basting brush. After 24 minutes, begin brushing the chicken on both sides, frequently turning and brushing on barbecue sauce until crispy and done. Serve with Maggie Cervantes' award winning potato or macaroni salad.

Note: Jane and her husband, Bob Motzinger, had adopted a houseful of children in the 1980s. This recipe was a favorite among her growing family and church friends in Scottsdale, Arizona.

CHAMPAGNE BRUNCH PUNCH 🍷

Bro. Joseph
Serves 20

2 bottles dry champagne,
 "Veuve Clicquot Brut" or
 "Perrier Jouet Brut"
1 cup brandy
32 oz. Perrier French imported
 sparkling water
1 bottle of Sautérne wine
¼ cup sugar
1 pint strawberries, wash, dry,
 and remove tops
1 bunch green grapes, wash,
 dry, and remove stems

Fill a heart-shaped mold or bunt cake mold half full with water. Place fruit in the mold the night before, add more water and freeze solid. When ready to serve, combine all other ingredients in a large punch bowl and stir. De-mold and float ice and fruit in punch bowl. Be sure to make all your ingredients very cold before mixing and serving this punch.

Note: Sautérnes is a French sweet wine from the Sautérnais region of the Graves section in Bordeaux, France. Sautérnes is made from Sémillon, Sauvignon blanc, and Muscadelle grapes. This punch has been popular for decades at Sunday brunch, New Year's Eve parties, holiday get-togethers, weddings, and anniversaries.

EGGPLANT PARMESAN 🎀

Paul Grappo
Serves 6 - 8

2 medium eggplants, washed and thinly sliced	1 large bottle Parmesan cheese
1 recipe bolognese sauce	1 small bag Mozzarella cheese
1 onion thinly sliced	1 bottle Canola oil
1 pepper thinly sliced	4 cups flour
1 small zucchini thinly sliced	4 eggs scrambled, with a splash of milk

Preheat oven to 350 F. Heat a small amount of oil in a large nonstick frying pan. Dip slices of eggplant in egg mixture, flour mixture, and then fry golden brown a couple of minutes on each side. Place on paper towels and set aside until all are done. Next, Pam spray a 9" x 13" glass baking dish. Place a layer of sauce on the bottom, layer eggplant, zucchini, onion, green pepper, Parmesan cheese, salt, and pepper. Then spoon sauce over the layer. Now, start over with layers of eggplant, etc. End by spooning sauce over the top layer and Parmesan cheese. Bake 45 to 60 minutes, until hot and bubbly. For the last 5 minutes, scatter the Mozzarella cheese on top and bake until melted. Remove from the oven and let rest 15 minutes before slicing into squares. Serve with a side of sauce, Parmesan, meatballs, salad, Italian bread, and red pepper flakes.

Note: Paula made this for decades by popular demand for family, as well as my father's coworkers. They would often eat Sunday leftovers at the office, made into an Italian sandwich and heated in mega factory ovens in the Pittsburgh area steel mills.

FRENCH RICE SALAD 🌐
(Salade de riz Française)

Kadir
Serves 4 - 6

2 cups rice cooked "al dente" according to directions
1 stalk celery chopped
1 carrot, peeled and chopped
1 small onion, peeled and minced
1 handful fresh parsley or basil, washed, dried, and minced
1 large tomato chopped
1 can corn, chilled and drained
2 tablespoons French or American mustard
Olive oil, Canola oil, and Apple Cider vinegar to taste
Sea salt and fresh ground pepper to taste
1 small green bell pepper chopped (optional)

Rinse the rice in cold water and drain well. Combine all ingredients in a large salad bowl and toss 25 to 50 times with mustard, oil, vinegar, salt, and pepper to taste. Chill in the refrigerator at least one hour or over night before serving. Goes great with summertime, large family gatherings, picnics, and barbecues. With no mayonnaise in the recipe, it can safely display on a buffet table for hours.

Note: Kadir was a chef from the Mideast working at a Christian youth hostile in the 1970s. It was on La rue de Musset, a very small street in the 16 arrondissement of Paris, France. He had a way of using leftovers from the day before and turning them into something special. This rice salad is one of the recipes where he really shows off his culinary skills.

GERMAN POTATO SALAD ⟩
(No Mayonnaise Potato Salad)

Bro. Joseph
Serves 4 - 6

6 to 8 potatoes, parboiled and chilled (optional to remove skins)
1 small white, yellow or red onion minced
2 sticks celery sliced
2 carrots (optional), peeled and chopped

¼ to ⅓ cup canola and/or olive oil combination
¼ to ⅓ cup apple cider or red wine vinegar
⅓ cup brown sugar
Sea salt and fresh ground pepper to taste

Be sure to cook the potatoes whole the night before "al dente." Don't overcook. Chill overnight. Next day cut potatoes into bite-size squares (peeling is optional). Then, in a large mixing bowl toss all ingredients together gently—about 25 to 50 times. Place in a medium salad bowl and chill until ready to serve. In the winter, this potato salad is also served warm with a beef roast or pork chops.

Note: German potato salad is perfect for summertime picnics, buffets, and outdoor events. With no mayonnaise in the recipe, it can safely stay for hours without refrigeration. Best of all, it's authentically German cuisine and tastes great with barbecues and summer fun. Try it in the winter as a side dish with pot roast or pan-seared pork chops.

ITALIAN BARBECUE SAUCE ⊘

James Grappo
Serves 6 - 8

1 large can tomato sauce
1 small onion and 4 cloves garlic, minced and sautéed in olive oil
1 tablespoon dried oregano
1 tablespoon dried basil
½ cup olive oil
¼ cup red wine vinegar
¼ cup brown sugar
Sea salt and pepper to taste
1 teaspoon American or French mustard

In a sauce pan, combine all ingredients and simmer on low for 5 minutes. Refrigerate and use the next day. Fire up the barbecue and arrange 2 to 3 pounds of chicken pieces on the grill. Now, using tongs, as you turn—sprinkle each side with the following: oregano, basil, garlic salt, onion salt, and pepper. Once fully seasoned over 20 minutes of turning and grilling, begin to baste the chicken heavily with a brush and barbecue sauce. The chicken is barbecued and ready to serve when the meat separates from the bone and no pink is visible.

Note: Jim Grappo Sr. invented this barbecue sauce and it became the standard at family gatherings for decades. Usually, he would also grill some sliced bread brushed with melted butter and garlic powder or salt. Along with corn on the cob, salad, and other side dishes, the barbecue was always a hit. Enjoy!

MEXICAN BEANS AND CHILI ⊘
(Chili Con Carne)

Maggie Cervantes
Serves 6 - 8

2 to 3 cups beef bouillon broth
½ lb. sautéed chorizo (pork)
1 30-oz. can red kidney beans with juice
1 lb. sautéed ground beef
1.5 lbs. prepared dried pinto beans cooked in plenty of water with salt and pepper
1 large onion chopped finely
o2 tablespoons garlic powder
½ teaspoon ground cumin
1 small can tomatoes chopped
¼ cup chili powder (New Mexico)

In a large sauce pot, sauté beef and chorizo. Then add onions, garlic, salt (to taste), tomatoes, chili powder, pinto beans (with a little juice), cumin, kidney beans with juice, and broth. Simmer 45 minutes adding more broth and chili powder if desired.

Note: Chili con carne was first introduced at the Chicago World Fair in 1893, along with the debut of caramelized popcorn (Cracker Jacks) and Aunt Jemima pancakes and maple syrup. The Chicago Fair celebrated the 400th anniversary of Christopher Columbus's arrival in the New World in 1492.

ORANGE SHERBET CELEBRATION PUNCH ★
(Nonalcoholic)

Bro. Joseph
Serves 20

2 cups water
2 cups sugar
1 cup pineapple juice
2 cups apricot nectar
1 cup orange juice

½ cup Real Lemon bottled concentrate
1 quart Ginger ale or Sprite
2 pints orange or pineapple sherbet

One day before, boil sugar and water—and cool. Mix with all ingredients except soda pop and ice cream. Cover and store in the refrigerator overnight. When ready to serve, stir well, and then pour into a large punch bowl—adding soda pop and ice cream. Enjoy!

Note: This Celebration Punch is always a hit with big and little kids, especially at birthdays and holiday parties!

POPCORN FRESH POPPED ◎
(Cheesy Herb Popcorn)

Bro. Joseph
Serves 2 - 4

½ cup Orville Redenbacher's popcorn
¼ cup vegetable oil
Garlic Salt
Onion Salt

½ cup Parmesan Cheese
Dried Oregano
Dried Basil
½ stick butter melted (optional)

In a medium sauce pan, add oil and popcorn, tilting and swirling until all the popcorn is coated with oil. Cover and simmer on medium-high heat. Once the corn begins to pop, place one hand on top of the lid and the other hand on the handle—holding it tight while lightly moving the pan back and forth over the heat to prevent burning in one spot. Once the popcorn reduces to one pop every few seconds, it is time to remove from the stove. Carefully pour popped popcorn in a large mixing bowl. Quickly drizzle butter and cheese over the top layer of the popcorn and then add onion, garlic salt, and herbs to taste. If you like a little hot spice, red cayenne pepper is a nice addition. Mix well by hand and serve in small bowls with your favorite soda or glass of cold beer.

Note: Native Americans first discovered popcorn millenniums ago in Guatemala or Mexico. Families have been enjoying popcorn together for thousands of years!

POTATO SALAD 🎀
(Best-ever Traditional Potato Salad)

Maggie Cervantes
Serves 4 - 6

1 medium Russet potato, boiled (not too soft) and cool to room temperature
6 eggs, hard-boiled and chopped
8 radishes chopped
3 celery sticks chopped
4 green onions thinly sliced
1 small can sliced black olives
¼ cup dill pickle juice
1 large dill pickled chopped
1 cup (or more) Best Foods Mayonnaise
1 heaping tablespoon mustard
Sea salt and pepper to taste
Paprika

In a large mixing bowl, toss potatoes, mayonnaise, dill pickle juice, mustard, salt, and pepper to taste. Fold in the vegetables and ½ of the chopped eggs. Pour into a serving bowl and top with the rest of the eggs. Garnish the top with sprinkles of paprika.

Note: Maggie's potato salad is always the best! Use this same recipe for her award-winning macaroni salad. Just substitute the potatoes for one box of elbow noodles cooked "Al Dente," chilled in cold water and drained well.

RAINBOW PINK PUNCH ★

Bro. Joseph
Serves 20

2 pints rainbow sherbet
1 12-oz. can frozen pink lemonade
2 10-oz. bags frozen raspberries
½ cup sugar
4 cups water
1 large bottle of Sprite or 7-Up

The night before, in a large pitcher or bowl, mix together all ingredients except for the soda pop and sherbet. Next day, when ready to serve, stir and pour into a large punch bowl. Combine all ingredients, including the soda pop and rainbow sherbet.

Note: For decades, Rainbow Pink Punch has been popular for teen parties, school girls party sleepovers, children's birthday parties, and festive family gatherings. Enjoy!

REFRESHING MINT PINEAPPLE PUNCH ★

Bro. Joseph
Serves 20
Nonalchoholic Party Beverage

6 cups sugar
4 cups water
2 cups mint leaves, freshly washed
3 quarts of ice

2 large cans pineapple juice
4 quarts Sprite or 7 Up
3 cups Real Lemon bottled concentrate

In a saucepan, boil water and sugar to dissolve and form light syrup. Remove from the heat and add the mint leaves. Let soak for 10 minutes. Discard leaves and combine all ingredients in a large punch bowl. Add extra ice as needed.

Note: This punch is excellent for weddings, anniversaries, and other special occasions—when you really want to wow the guests!

SUMMER FRESH FRUIT SALAD

Bro. Joseph
Serves 8

4 cups watermelon, cubed and seeded
2 cups strawberries sliced
2 large peaches cubed
2 large nectarines cubed
1 cup seedless grapes cut in half
1 cup fresh blueberries or blackberries

1 lemon
¼ cup mint leaves finely minced
2 heaping tablespoons honey
1 to 2 splashes of Grande Manier or Limoncello (optional)

Place all ingredients in a large mixing bowl. Set aside and then make the dressing. In a small bowl, mix together (using a whisk) juice of one lemon, ¼ cup finely minced mint, 2 heaping tablespoons of honey, and a splash of Grande Manier (optional). Mix well. Pour over fruit salad and chill for one hour or overnight.

Note: Whether you are trying to beat the heat of summer or prepare for a graduation party, a picnic, or some other family gathering, a fresh fruit salad chilled to perfection will make you the hit of the party.

ZUCCHINI STICKS

Angela Chavez

⅔ cup **Italian Parmesan Cheese**
½ cup **Progresso seasoned bread crumbs**
2 **large eggs lightly beaten**
5 **medium zucchini, washed and ends cut off**
Canola oil

In a shallow bowl, combine the cheese and bread crumbs. In another shallow bowl, beat eggs. Cut zucchini in half crosswise, then lengthwise into quarters. Add zucchini to eggs and coat by hand gently. Lift out one stick at a time and roll in cheese/bread mixture to coat evenly. Repeat until all zucchini sticks are coated. Lay sticks slightly apart on a Pam sprayed cookie sheet. Drizzle oil over zucchini. Bake, uncovered, for 25 minutes at 450 F until coating is well browned and crusty. It's tasty as a holiday appetizer or side dish for a family barbecue or picnic!

INDEX OF RECIPES

APPETIZERS & BEVERAGES

AVOCADO DIP	1
CELERY APPETIZER PLATTER	2
CUCUMBER YOGURT SAUCE	2
EGGPLANT APPETIZER	3
GARBANZO BEAN DIP	4
HOMEMADE COUGH SYRUP	4
HOMEMADE YOGURT	5
ITALIAN OLIVES	5
LUPINI BEANS	6
OLIVE APPETIZER	7
ORANGE LEMONADE	8
ROASTED RED PEPPERS	9
SHRIMP COCKTAIL	9
STUFFED DATES	0
STUFFED MUSHROOMS	0
SWEET AND SOUR MEATBALLS	11
WATERMELON FETA CHEESE APPETIZER	2

SOUPS & SALADS

BEEF VEGETABLE SOUP	3
BEET SALAD	4
BLACK BEAN CUBAN SALAD	5
CABBAGE AND WHITE BEAN SOUP	6
DANDELION SALAD	7
ITALIAN BREAD BEAN SOUP	18
LENTIL SOUP	19
PARSLEY SALAD OF LEBANON	20
PASTA AND BEANS SOUP	21
PEAR SALAD FOR FALL	22
SALAD WITH TUNA	23
SUISSE CARROT SALAD	24
TOMATO SALAD	24
WEDDING SOUP	25
WINTER TOMATO SALAD	26

VEGETABLES & SIDE DISHES

APPLE CHUTNEY	27
BEANS AND GREENS	28
CABBAGE AND POTATOES	29
CANDIED YAMS	29
CHINESE FRIED RICE	30
CORN CASSEROLE	31
CORN FRITTERS	31
CORNMEAL FRIED	32
CRANBERRY CHUTNEY	32
CRANBERRY RASPBERRY RELISH	33
CUCUMBER FREEZER PICKLES	33
FRESH CRANBERRY RELISH	34
HOMINY	34
MEXICAN FRIED RICE	35
NOODLES AND CREAM CHEESE	35
PEAS AND EGGS	36
PEAS & PEARL ONIONS	36
PEAS CREAMED	37
PINEAPPLE STUFFING	37
PLANTAINS	38
POTATO PANCAKES	39
POTATOES MASHED WITH GARLIC	39
POTATOES PAN-FRIED	40
POTATOES ROSEMARY	40
RAISIN SAUCE	41
RICE PERFECT	41
SCALLOPED POTATOES	42
SPINACH CREAMED	42
VEGETABLE MEDLEY	43

MAIN DISHES

BEEF BRISKET OVEN ROASTED	45
BEEF ROAST IN RED WINE	46
BEEF ROAST SWEET AND SAUCY	47
BEEF TENDERLOIN STEAKS	47
CHICKEN KOREAN	48
CHICKEN ROSEMARY	49
CHIMICHURRI SAUCE	50
CHRISTMAS AND EASTER BAKED HAM	51
ENCHILADAS	51
FISH PAN-SEARED	52
IRISH OATMEAL BOWL	53
ITALIAN FRIED CHICKEN	54
ITALIAN PIZZA	55
MEATLOAF AMERICAN STYLE	56
PASTA AND MEATBALLS	57

Ordering St. Joseph's Table Cookbook

Cookbooks make great gifts for birthdays, anniversaries, weddings, showers, Christmas, Easter, Mother's Day, and other special occasions. To order additional copies of *St. Joseph's Table Cookbook*, detach and mail the order form below with a check or money order to:

Servants of the Father of Mercy, Inc. - Mercy Books
1544 MORSE AVE STE A, VENTURA, CA 93003
(310) 595-4175
Or order at our website www.ServantsoftheFather.org

. . . .

Please send me _____ copies of:
St. Joseph's Table Cookbook
at **$29.95** donation to help the 80,000 + homeless and small **gift** s/h per book.
Enclosed is my check for $_____.

Mail book(s) to:

_____
Name

_____
Address

_____   _____   _____
City   State   Zip

(_____) _____   _____
Phone   E-mail

Made in United States
Troutdale, OR
06/07/2024

20383825R00076